MW01173502

Be Your Own Management Consultant

Be Your Own Management Consultant

MARK PINDER AND
STUART McADAM

FINANCIAL TIMES

PITMAN PUBLISHING

PITMAN PUBLISHING
128 Long Acre, London WC2E 9AN

A Division of Longman Group UK Limited

© Mark Pinder and Stuart McAdam, 1994

First published in Great Britain 1994

British Library Cataloguing in Publication Data
A CIP catalogue record for this book can be obtained from the British Library.

ISBN 0 273 60466 X

All rights reserved; no part of this publication may be reproduced, stored
in a retrieval system, or transmitted in any form or by any means, electronic,
mechanical, photocopying, recording, or otherwise without either the prior
written permission of the Publishers or a licence permitting restricted copying
in the United Kingdom issued by the Copyright Licensing Agency Ltd,
90 Tottenham Court Road, London W1P 9HE. This book may not be lent,
resold, hired out or otherwise disposed of by way of trade in any form
of binding or cover other than that in which it is published, without the
prior consent of the Publishers.

Phototypeset in Linotron Times Roman
by Northern Phototypesetting Co. Ltd., Bolton
Printed and bound in Great Britain
by Biddles Ltd., Guildford and King's Lynn

It is the Publishers' policy is to use paper manufactured from sustainable forests.

CONTENTS

ACKNOWLEDGEMENTS

We would like to thank the following for their assistance, encouragement and advice:
Pani Pinderova, Norma Bastos, Sue Wells, David Williams, Tony MacGregor, Julian Soltau and John Morley.

1

WHY YOU DON'T NEED A CONSULTANT . . . AND WHY YOU DO

What is 'internal consulting'? In what ways is it different from external consulting – and in what ways is it the same? Above all, what benefits can be obtained from it, and how can an organisation go about gaining these benefits?

USING EXTERNAL CONSULTANTS

Many people have had the experience of using external consultants. In some cases, this has been a positive experience; the consultants have brought a fresh insight to some key problem, or have worked effectively with client staff to achieve real, meaningful results and benefits. In other cases, their involvement has been less successful, to the extent that clients question the value of ever using them again. The following is a selection of typical client views sometimes heard about external consultants:

> *'They came in and spent eighteen months working with us just to tell me something I already knew.'*

> *'What they said was fine, but it was too peripheral – it didn't really address the key issues facing our business.'*

> *'They didn't liaise well with my own staff: just came in, gave us a fat report, then went away again. Things have moved on since then. I*

was expecting them to pass on some of their skills and experience, so we could address our problems on an ongoing basis.'

'I thought they were more interested in selling us another piece of work, than completing the one we'd already contracted for them to do.'

'The people who came in and did the work were different from the ones I met when we were negotiating the contract. I didn't like that – I felt I was being fobbed off with lower grade, less experienced people.'

'They did some good work, but what a cost! You know the joke about why a consultant is like a rhino? They're both thick skinned and know how to charge.'

There are all sorts of reasons why the relationship between consultant and client can break down. In some cases, it may be that the consultant is not competent to do the job, or that they simply haven't devoted enough time and effort to it. But this is rare – most consultants are competent, conscientious people who take their work seriously and genuinely want to give their clients good value. More frequently, the problems are there at the outset, and relate mostly to a lack of understanding between consultant and client about what is needed and what is being offered. In the worst cases, this gap in understanding widens as the project develops, until in the end everybody knows the outcome isn't what was expected in the first place (though nobody can remember exactly what **was** expected in the first place).

This is, of course, the 'worst case' scenario, and the majority of consulting projects don't go as badly wrong as that: but the point is that it is poor communication, most frequently, that leads to poor consulting work. Fig. 1.1 illustrates why this is so.

The three critical success factors of a consulting project (shown in Fig. 1.1 as the three points of the triangle) **must** be in synergy at the outset if progress is to be made towards successful completion:

● **what you want** is the perception that you, the client, have of your problem and how it should be solved. You may, of course, have

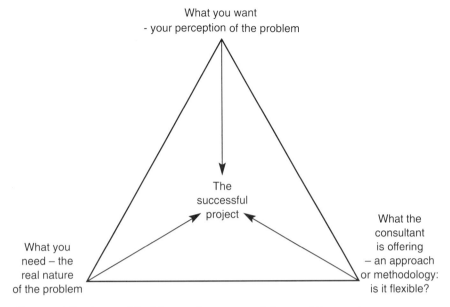

What you want
- your perception of the problem

The
successful
project

What you
need – the
real nature
of the problem

What the
consultant
is offering
– an approach
or methodology:
is it flexible?

Fig. 1.1 The three critical factors in a successful consulting project

only a vague, general notion of the best solution: that, after all, is what you're paying the consultant for: But at the very least, you need to be able to articulate the nature of your problem and in what way you want things to be different. If you who know your business best can't do this, how can you expect the consultants to understand it?

● **What the consultant is offering** is independence, professionalism, round-the-clock client care . . . at least that's what your consultant will tell you! In most cases he or she will be telling the truth, but you, the client, should be looking for more than this. You should be looking for evidence of previous success, flexibility in approach, and above all evidence that the consultant is genuinely capable of forming a sound understanding of your business issues and of developing meaningful solutions that will work. Many consultants have developed standard approaches and methodologies to client issues which, having served them well in the past, form the cornerstone of their work. There is nothing wrong in this, as long as the approach can be adapted to suit the individual needs of your business.

- **What you need** may be (though not necessarily) very different from what you want. Consider the following example:

The client, a retail finance company that had recently been through a merger, was having problems with its staff. Increasingly, people were expressing dissatisfaction with the grades they were in, and their status relative to other staff they regarded as their equals but who came from the other merger partner. The company decided it wanted a new job evaluation scheme. A firm of management consultants was brought in, who designed and implemented a new job evaluation system that was fair, rigorous and implemented a common grading structure. The company received even more complaints about pay and grading than it had before.

The problem was this: a new job evaluation scheme was what the company **wanted**, but not what it **needed**. The consultants were technically competent and dedicated to their task, but they made no attempt to question the client as to the real nature of the problem (an easy trap to fall into with a large contract at stake). Had they done so they would have realised that the root of the problem was staff motivation and the lack of progress made at integrating the staff of the two former entities following the merger. Unless these issues were addressed, it was inevitable that disquiet concerning status and grade would continue.

The sort of problems illustrated above can occur whether the consultants used are 'internal' or 'external'. There are however, many circumstances where the use of trained and technically competent internal consultants, who should have a much deeper understanding of the culture and circumstances of the organisation, will produce better results. Before considering these circumstances, it will be useful to consider the approach taken by professional consulting firms to winning, managing and completing client engagements.

HOW CONSULTANTS WIN THEIR BUSINESS

A major issue for external consultants is that they have divided loyalties. On one hand there is you, the client, who is paying the fees and is entitled to receive expert, independent advice that will benefit your business. On the other there is the consultants employer (maybe one of the 'big six' accounting firms, maybe a smaller, specialist, 'niche' consultancy) which may place limits on the amount of time spent on a project, and will measure its consultants' success, at least in part, in terms of factors such as new business generated and ability to stay within budget. This issue has a major impact on how consultants approach new clients.

Gaining an entry

There are many different ways in which consultants can acquire new business. These include:

- marketing events, such as roundtables, workshops or 'business breakfasts', to which existing or potential clients are invited. Frequently the organisers will publicise a particular product or approach they have developed, and will leave plenty of publicity material (brochures, magazine articles etc.) lying around. In other cases consultants make presentations at conferences organised by professional associations or academic institutions. Whatever the precise circumstances, you can be sure that the delegate list will be carefully scrutinised and delegates can expect to receive 'follow-up' material after the event. This may include an invitation to lunch with a partner of the firm or other luminary to explore areas of common interest.
- personal contacts, which may come through the consultants business or personal life. Many consultants join professional associations or local business groups and cultivate potential clients from these sources.
- the targeting of specific business sectors or companies that are seen as 'key' target clients. Having identified the target, approaches towards them can be highly imaginative: many consulting firms do not approve of 'cold calling', and as a result are obliged to create some pretext for making the initial approach and then sustaining the relationship.
- cross-selling: particularly amongst the composite firms with

accounting and tax practices, many leads come from other parts of the business. Winning projects with existing audit clients is usually easier than where there is no previous relationship. A difficulty from the consultants point of view is that auditors can be particularly nervous about letting consultants loose on their own hard-won client list.

- former colleagues are another relatively easy source of business. Many bigger consulting firms expect a high staff turnover amongst their professional staff, and actively keep contact with these 'alumni' who move on to take up management positions in commerce and industry.

- invitations to tender: many large-scale projects are sponsored by development banks and funding agencies, which invite consultants to propose for work. Invitations are issued to consulting firms registered with them to carry out relevant work.

- brochures, newsletters, magazine articles written by consultants, and other published material is often used actively to target clients. Many consultancies issue such material regularly to existing and potential clients, to keep them advised of recent developments and try to attract business in new areas.

Any of these different activities can lead to an enquiry – where the consultant is, one way or another, invited to suggest how they might carry out a specific piece of work for the client. The door has been opened: and in some cases, the consultant may have been at work on a key target client for years and years to reach this stage. So – having made the opening, how does the consultant respond?

Meetings, proposals and presentations

In most cases, initially, by finding out as much as possible about the client and the nature of the job they are hoping to win. This is likely to involve an initial meeting to discuss the background and needs, and tease out the key issues involved. The meeting will probably have other objectives, including: demonstrating professional credibility; establishing rapport with the client; identifying the 'key players' in the organisation; finding out if there are any competitors for the work, and who they are; and gaining a feel for the likely scope of the project, including the timescale and budget. The consultant may not be open about these objectives, but it is as important for the client as for the consultant that they are achieved. There is no point, for example, in the consultant selling the benefits of a piece of work to a person who cannot influence whether it goes ahead or not, or having an unrealistic view of the scope of the work involved. Remember the need for understanding, on both sides and at the outset, if the thing is to be a success. It is likely the consultant will follow other lines of research, such as obtaining textline articles about the client, reading previous annual reports and talking to colleagues who have had previous contact. However the initial client meeting is usually the most important means of establishing a real feel for the clients requirements.

If the consultants have done the job properly, by the time they prepare a written proposal they should have established a clear understanding of the task in hand. Proposals come in many different forms and sizes. In some cases, a one or two page letter, covering the gist of a previous conversation with the client, is sufficient. In others, the proposal will be a full-blown report in its own right, running to many pages of text, making use of flowcharts and diagrams to illustrate aspects of the work and perhaps with a separate volume of appendices or CVs. At the very least, the proposal should include the following details:

- a brief summary of the background to the project;
- a description of the client's requirements (as the consultant understands them to be);
- a description of the approach the consultant will take in carrying out the project;
- an indication of the amount of consulting time involved and the overall elapsed timescale;
- details of the staff who will carry out the work and what their roles will be;
- the fees that will be charged (including any direct costs such as travel, accommodation and report preparation); and
- most importantly, the outcome and deliverables of the project,

highlighting the main benefits.

A consultant proposal is, at once, a marketing tool (an opportunity to demonstrate capability to do the job, understanding of the client's business, etc.) and a contractual document formally stating how the consultant will carry out the project should they win the contract. It is, therefore, a document of fundamental importance, which can be referred to, at a later date, by the consultant or the client to ensure that the terms of reference of the project are adhered to. It should be studied in detail at the outset, and **any** areas of misunderstanding clarified before any decision is taken to award the contract! Remember, at this stage the consultant is still trying to sell their services and there will inevitably be the temptation to put into the proposal more than they are able to deliver. It goes without saying that any negotiations on price or length of contract should be concluded before the work actually begins.

Client presentations play a key part in winning business for consultants, especially where the project is open for competitive tendering. Few consultants enjoy 'beauty parades', in which the tenderers are wheeled in before the client one after another to make their formal declarations of how they would do the job and why they would do it better than any of their competitors. Despite the fact that they are likely to be highly trained in effective presentation skills, consultants can be as nervous before a critical audience as anyone else. In fact, consultant presentations are usually highly accomplished affairs, making good use of overhead slides and other visual aids that are appropriate. A good presentation will have been rehearsed beforehand, will involve all members of the proposed project team and will give ample opportunity for questions (many of which will have been anticipated in advance). Any presentation that is wide of the mark in terms of client expectation should be regarded with suspicion; this is a strong indication that the consultant hasn't prepared thoroughly and doesn't have a true understanding of the clients business issues and requirements.

Key messages

An internal consultant is unlikely to have to be as proactive in seeking and winning work as an external consultant. Indeed, it is possible that many people reading the previous few pages will be surprised (even horrified) by some of the tactics that consultants use and will wonder how relevant these are to their own circumstances. However, there are a number of key messages arising from the ways external consultants seek and win their business that are highly relevant to the process of internal consulting. In particular:

- even for internal consultants, there is likely to be a need to market their services internally. If people within the organisation are unaware of how you can help them, how can you expect them to give you work? Remember, your 'clients' are unlikely to be your 'line' managers in a traditional sense, and there is no obligation on them to make use of your support.
- it follows on from this that the internal consultant needs to establish credibility with potential clients. This will come largely through the evidence of good work previously done, technical and professional competence and understanding of the business. It may be necessary to carry out research to establish full understanding and 'appear credible'. It is equally important to establish contact with the people in the organisation who can genuinely commission consulting work.
- the project details **must** be discussed and agreed in detail with the client in advance. Failure to establish complete understanding as to the nature of the project and the desired outcome may cause considerable problems later; in extreme cases an unresolvable dispute between client and consultant as to what was intended.
- the terms of reference for a possible project should be explored thoroughly and presented in a formal proposal. It is simply not acceptable for any consultant to cut corners in this area. Again, to do so is likely to cause major problems.
- for internal as well as external consultants, there is a range of key consulting skills associated with winning projects, and it is essential that the internal consultant learns these skills. They include the techniques of proposal writing, scoping of projects and making effective presentations.

HOW CONSULTANTS MANAGE PROJECTS

A former consulting colleague, well known for his wry remarks concerning his profession, once remarked that 'all projects have four phases, because five would be too many and three too few.' Unfair, perhaps, but indicative of the highly structured approach taken by many consultants to their clients. In most cases, a consulting project is a finite piece of work, based on carefully worded and agreed terms of reference and with the deliverables clearly specified. In theory, this should mean that carrying out the project is simply a matter of following the agreed approach through to its logical conclusion. In practice, things rarely work out like this. Sometimes, the balance between client expectation and what the consultant means to deliver is wrong. Issues arise along the way that put the consultant under pressure, and for which there is no time allocated in the budget. For example the client may discover that they require something more, or something different from what they originally wanted. Whatever the case, navigating a way through those four phases and bringing the project to a conclusion can call for a good deal of skill and dexterity. Some of the key facets of effective project management are set out below.

Research/investigation

All good projects are founded on sound, wide-ranging research. One of the major benefits a client can gain from employing consultants is finding out about 'best practice' and what other organisations, including their competitors, are doing in a particular area. Equally, it is important for the consultants to gain a sound understanding of what is going on within the client organisation if they are to bring an incisive, independent approach, as well as an awareness of the latest products, technical developments or management thinking that are relevant.

Research can be carried out in many ways, including interviews, questionnaires, scrutiny of reports and published information, textline searches, etc. Needless to say, all information gained should be properly recorded so that it is accessible and can be analysed thoroughly as the project moves towards recommendation stage. The essential thing is that all information from both external and internal sources can be drawn together and presented properly to the benefit of the client.

Key message: why can't internal consultants carry out research as effectively as external consultants? Some would argue that they are not sufficiently independent to do so, or that they don't have the resources (resourcefulness?) to obtain wide-ranging information. These arguments are largely spurious: in most cases there is no reason why a suitably trained internal consultant cannot be sufficiently detached from his or her internal client, or cannot obtain all information necessary to carry out a project effectively.

Client meetings and presentations

These are essential to update the client throughout the project, and gain feedback which will help steer the work to its conclusion. Many projects have provision in the budget for regular progress reports, often on a weekly basis, which tend to be informal, one-to-one meetings between consultant and the client. Sometimes, more formal meetings will be required, for example to present findings to a wider range of client staff who may not be aware of details of the work done and may need convincing about the benefits. These are often held as workshop sessions in which the consultant facilitates an open discussion and records the key messages coming through. Use can be made of overhead slides, flipcharts and other presentation material to ensure clarity and generate quality input.

Key message: don't underestimate the value of meetings and presentations, they are a vital component of any consulting engagement, whether internal or external. There is no better way of ensuring real understanding and generation of valuable opinions and ideas.

'Consultant, manage thyself'

Some consultants (especially more senior ones) are terrible at managing their own time. They get away with it by convincing everyone that a) they are frantically busy all of the time, and b) their time is so valuable that you, the client, should be glad of every bit of it you can get. Sometimes, they are late for 'or even miss altogether' important client meetings. They are always on the move, when you think they are in Birmingham they are on the plane for Budapest. Altogether, they create havoc amongst the more ordered beings who have to cover for them in one way or another, and are the despair of their consulting colleagues.

This is all very well if you are a recognised guru in your chosen field, or your clients are so in awe of you that they simply accept erratic behaviour as a symptom of your superior intellect. Otherwise, you are in danger of being dumped very rapidly! There are some simple rules to follow:

- never exceed your budget (unless you have negotiated an extension with your client);
- always produce written reports on time;
- never promise more than you can deliver;
- if you encounter difficulties with your timescales, ensure your client knows about it as soon as possible;
- above all, never, **never** miss client meetings!

Managing staff

For bigger engagements the usual arrangement is for a senior consultant to act as project manager, while more junior consultants carry out the field work. The project manager will be predominantly responsible for client liaison and controlling the work of the others. This will involve setting and monitoring their budgets, ensuring that their work meets quality standards and adds value to the project as a whole, and leading project team meetings. Project management is a very demanding role. Frequently, the consultants are technical experts in their own right, whereas the manager may have less knowledge in their specialist area, making it difficult to question the quality of their input. Management styles vary considerably, from the autocrat who drives his consultants to distraction (and sometimes to tears), to almost complete detachment from the detailed reports and other work being submitted as part of the project. An approach somewhere between the two extremes is best in most circumstances, although ultimately a lot depends on the skill and commitment of the consultants being managed.

Another aspect of project management is making use of client counterpart staff. It is essential, if the benefits of the consulting approach are to be passed on to the client, that counterparts are integrated into the team and given meaningful roles that contribute to the result. This is a real failing in many projects. Too often, clients are treated purely as the passive recipients of the consultants' advice, who have little or no say in the recommendations (all too frequently, they are regarded with secret contempt as well) and who must simply accept the outcome of the project. Real consulting requires that the client is brought into the decision-making process and above all is empowered to carry the recommendations forward through involvement in all the issues, principles and objectives that have emerged throughout the duration of the project.

Key message: don't become too detached from your client. It *is* possible to involve them, without jeopardising independence. In the internal consulting context, this may mean making use of staff from the business or department that has commissioned your work, in all kinds of activities from research through to decision-making. Active involvement of client staff will ensure 'buy-in' to the work and will considerably improve the probability of recommendations being carried though to implementation.

Managing client expectations

This is a key aspect of overall project management, and something that can be done through client involvement. Many consultants are careful to record in writing decisions made and agreements reached during the project, so these can be referred to later. Many consultants are also very prone to reminding their clients of the precise contents of the original proposal, whenever they show signs of forgetting or deviating from what was originally agreed.

A particular issue for consultants is 'scope creep'. This occurs when the client shows signs of wanting something more than was originally agreed. Up to a point it is not a problem (after all, many consultants pride themselves on giving their clients more than they could expect) but where the additional work required will be substantial it is necessary to tackle the matter quickly and head-on. Usually, if the client is 'trying it on', they will back down. If on the other hand the extra work has genuinely become necessary as a result of the project, there is an opportunity for the consultant to negotiate for additional time and fees to carry it out. This is quite a common way for consultants to gain additional business.

Another issue is that of bringing a project to its conclusion. For a variety of reasons, some clients can be reluctant to end their relationship with the consultant, with the result that a project can drag on with no sign off or any formal conclusion. This is unsatisfactory to both parties, and may require the consultant to arrange a 'sign-off' meeting at which final reports or other deliverables are formally handed over to the client.

Information analysis and report preparation

In terms of analysing information, it is particularly dangerous for a consultant to work in isolation. However good he or she may be at interpretation, it is inevitable that others will be able to give a different insight into problems and issues, and may highlight features that would otherwise be missed. Some consultants address projects with preconceived ideas about how to conduct them, and even what the final outcomes should be. None should be so arrogant as to dismiss the opinions, advice and technical expertise of other consultants and client staff.

As far as reports are concerned, another unfortunate tendency of some consultants is to produce massive, monolithic reports that stand no chance of being effectively read and interpreted by clients. This is seen as giving 'added value', which is almost literally measured by weight of paper. All too often, the heavyweight report is used as the justification for a project that has not met its objectives, either due to lack of client involvement or real investigation as to whether the recommendations made can really be implemented. While reports need to give the full picture, they should address the key issues and not burden the client down with unnecessary detail. Charts and diagrams should be used to clarify issues, not over-complicate them. In many consulting projects there is a strong case for doing away with written reports altogether and using other more direct, accessible methods of communicating issues and recommendations.

Key message: think of your written reports as a means of communication, not an end result. If your aim is to help your client, your reports should be presented with the purpose of clarifying, convincing, and facilitating change; not justifying your expensive and time-consuming involvement.

Delivering results

Having just said that reports should not be used as a stick to beat the client with, they are undoubtedly the most common form of project deliverable that consultants use; and a good report is indeed a very effective way of presenting findings and recommendations. Other methods of delivery include:

- presentations to the client (usually accompanied with hard copies of any slides used, for future reference). These can be very effective in gaining agreement to results and commitment to future action;
- a fully-developed method or system, including all necessary documents, equipment, materials and training required to implement the system;
- transfer of skills to managers or staff of the client organisation, for example through a series of training courses;
- research data which may be presented in 'raw' form or may have been analysed to extract key information;
- completion of a change project in which the consultant has been involved as a facilitator or adviser to the client's management team;
- a technical specification for implementation of new systems (for example, information technology or quality management).

This list illustrates the wide variety of project deliverables, which indeed reflects the widely varying nature of projects themselves. A good consultant will ensure that the deliverables are appropriate to the circumstances and, above all, leave the client with something tangible that will be of benefit to the development of their business.

Whatever the case, there are a number of rules to be observed in presenting deliverables. The most important are:

- they must take account of the client's ability to understand, interpret and, ultimately, take action on them;
- they must be on time, and should cover all commitments that were made in the original proposal,
- they should contain no surprises: any unexpected findings or turns taken during the project should have been brought to the clients attention well in advance of its conclusion.

Project review and appraisal

It is common practice within the bigger consulting firms for consultants to have a formal appraisal by their manager on completion of a project. This usually covers key aspects of the work done and focuses on different aspects of the consultant's performance such as analysis of information, work organisation, skill in handling client meetings, and teamworking. These appraisals can be of value to consultants in identifying strengths and weaknesses and consequent training needs.

Some consultants formally approach their clients on completion of a project for a review of how they performed. This too can be a very valuable way of finding out about strengths and weaknesses, and furthermore many clients appreciate it as evidence of professionalism and commitment. Even in the internal consulting context, client reviews can be a valuable tool for improving performance and maintaining rapport with people in the organisation who may, in the future, need further work from you.

Selling on

Any good consultant will always be looking to sell on further work to their clients, either by extending the projects they are working on or winning new projects in other areas. There is nothing wrong in this, often, consultants can identify a problem within the client organisation that the client is unaware of, and there can obviously be benefits to the client in developing a long-term relationship with a particular consultant.

A less healthy situation is where the consultant deliberately frames a proposal in such a way that, as the project develops, it becomes clear that further work will be required. Unfortunately this is quite a common approach taken by some consultants. Either a key aspect of the work will be omitted, or the approach taken will follow a direction that leads inevitably towards a secondary need that the consultant has the skills to meet. It is a high-risk strategy as there is always the possibility that the client might realise what is happening, or at least balk at the extra fees involved and lose faith.

Key message (for internal consultants): don't be shy to suggest that further work is necessary, where it genuinely is; but being less than open with your internal clients in order to gain a 'hook' to further work is a sharp practice that can seriously damage your reputation.
Key message (for clients): be as sure as possible, particularly in commissioning work with consultants you don't know, that there are no key omissions in the proposal that will cost you dear to rectify at a later date!

DIFFERENT TYPES OF CONSULTING

Consulting projects come in many different shapes and forms. Consider the following:

- developing a new organisation structure for an Eastern European telecommunications company. This involves detailed research into the existing structure and culture of the organisation, comparison with the structures of Western telecoms companies, the development of different organisation models, the testing of these to select the most appropriate model to the company in view of its objectives and level of technical development. Finally, production of a detailed report, including an implementation plan, for the benefit of the development banks sponsoring the project as much as the client itself.

- selecting an Information Technology (IT) supplier for a financial services company, requiring extensive liaison with potential suppliers, detailed analysis of the specifications of several different systems, and investigation into the implementation costs and other constraints before working with the client to select the best system.
- a series of management training courses for middle managers of a retail institution. In addition to the development and delivery of training modules, the client's own training staff are involved so that the skills and style of the training can be transferred. In addition to this skills transfer, the project deliverables include a full set of training material including role play exercises, trainers' notes and other supporting documents.
- a secondment with the client to facilitate a major change programme. Working with the chief executive and other senior managers, a programme is put in place and implemented over a period of six months. There is no paper-based 'deliverable' apart from a few notes and hard copies of presentation slides used during change management seminars.

This is just a small sample of some typical projects, covering the spectrum from research-based projects to 'process consulting': in which the consultant is acting in an advisory capacity almost as a member of the clients management team. As an internal consultant, it is possible you may become involved in projects at either end of the spectrum. As long as you have the right mix of skills, there is no reason why you can't do as good or better a job as an external consultant in many situations.

A key point here is that the consulting market is changing. Until recently, many clients commissioned consultants to carry out research projects in the main, and would not have considered using them in a quasi-internal context as advisers to management. As the pace of change has quickened in many organisations, however, and as questions are more frequently raised about the value of 'traditional-style' consulting projects, the demand for process consulting has grown to the extent that many clients now expect much more involvement from consultants in facilitating and implementing change and decision-making. Many external consultants have been slow to appreciate this shift in their market, or have proved incapable of handling the different demands of process consulting that, in many ways, are so different from their traditional way of doing things. This represents a major opportunity for the internal consultant.

In writing this book, we have assumed that the internal consultant may become involved in many different types of project, but that there is likely in most cases to be a strong 'process consulting' element requiring skills in areas such as negotiating, advising, implementing, adjusting, and managing the results of projects previously carried out.

THE BENEFITS OF EFFECTIVE PROCESS CONSULTING

Process consulting is defined as projects in which a consultant works closely with the client to develop recommendations and advice, and assist with the implementation of these. It can bring many benefits, which include:

- bringing independent thinking to problems and issues that otherwise would not be easily perceived by managers who are too closely involved and who 'cannot see the wood for the trees';
- achieving understanding of the practicalities and realities of issues that might not be understood if too theoretical an approach were applied;
- ensuring consistent interface between the consultant and client; again, something that does not always happen in many more theoretically-oriented consulting engagements;
- a greater sense of ownership and commitment from the consultant, through greater involvement in the implementation of new ideas and methods.

Arguably, these benefits can be obtained whether an internal or an external consultant is carrying out the project. However, there are potential advantages and disadvantages in using one or the other.

Independent thinking

An external consultant is likely to be more independent, although this will not necessarily be so. It is important for the internal consultant not to have a direct reporting relationship with the client, so that the client cannot use managerial muscle to exert influence. It should be possible, in most organisations, for the consultant to belong to a separate function with reporting lines that are well-removed from the influence of his or her clients, and to work with the understanding that any attempts to exert pressure will not be tolerated. Nevertheless, on this score one up for the external consultant.

Understanding the practicalities

This is an area where the internal consultant should have a distinct advantage: no external consultant, however dedicated and incisive, can really expect to know as much about the way the organisation works, thinks and acts. Knowing the organisation's strengths and limitations is a key factor in coming up with recommendations that can be translated into real, practical results.

Achieving consistent interface

Again, the internal consultant should have the edge here through knowledge of the organisation and the people involved. One of the most difficult tasks for an external consultant is to assess the attitudes and position in the structure – informal as well as formal – of client contacts. The internal consultant is also likely to be more readily available to address queries and problems that arise, and may more easily build up the level of rapport with clients that is essential to the success of process consulting projects.

Ownership and commitment

This is the area where the internal consultant should have the biggest advantage. However dedicated to their clients they are, external consultants will always have loyalties to their own employers and may therefore be pulled in different directions at any given time. In the worst situations, this may mean they are not available at critical times due to other commitments. They may also grow concerned about the implications for their professional careers of becoming too involved in the implementation of recommendations and back away. This can be a particular problem with work that is controversial, unpopular or carries a high risk of failure. If supported properly by the organisation, an internal consultant should be more prepared to support controversial decisions, maintain commitment through their implementation and take responsibility for the results.

In highlighting the advantage of using internal consultants to carry out work, we assume that these consultants are fully trained in the necessary technical skills and have the right attitudes and approach towards clients and their problems. Essentially, this book is intended to describe in detail these consulting competencies and how they can be acquired. It should be regarded as a starting point towards setting up a professional internal consulting practice with the objective of dealing more effectively with the key problems, issues and objectives of the organisation.

2

ESTABLISHING YOURSELF AS AN INTERNAL CONSULTANT

Because the internal consultant is operating from within the organisation rather than advising from outside, he or she is subject to different tensions and pressures than the external consultant. This is not to say that the technical skills required to carry out projects are greatly different between the two: however the **attitudes** required are somewhat different. This is particularly so when the consultant role is combined with other roles involving line management responsibilities. 'Getting started' can also be more difficult for an internal consultant. When one is buried within a large and diverse organisation, how does one go about building a presence, become known to key managers and differentiate oneself from the persuasive approaches of external consulting firms?

THE CONSULTING CONTEXT

The precise circumstances of an internal consultant within an organisation may vary considerably:

- you may be operating as part of an autonomous consulting unit: many large organisations have established such units within their structures, in recognition that line managers need recourse to specialist technical skills to address business issues. You are part of a multi-disciplinary group, which may be called upon to undertake projects in many different areas. Teamworking with other consultants in the group is therefore very important. Your project work is carried out in a genuine client/consultant context, i.e. there is no direct line reporting to the managers who are your internal clients.

- you may be a specialist consultant within a function such as IT, Marketing or Human Resources, giving advice to managers in a specific technical area. Sometimes, consulting roles of this type are combined with a line management role which can, if not handled properly, cause conflict.
- you may be operating as a 'sole practitioner', probably giving advice in a specific technical area but independent from any line management function. This may mean that you have no staff resources of your own, but need to call upon staff elsewhere in the organisation to help you with project work. There is likely to be a strong emphasis on project management of such staff rather than self management. It is also likely that you will be allied to the top management of the organisation (who will be the sponsors of your work and have the clout to allocate resources to specific projects).
- in most cases, you will carry out work for the organisation only, and your budgets and pricing policy will reflect this. Sometimes, however, you may be required to seek work from external clients, or may identify a market niche which makes it possible to sell your services to external organisations.

All of these circumstances differ from those of an external consultant in one key respect; because you are within the organisation, you can't just walk away from the results of your recommendations and find another client. This places you under greater pressure to deliver results that bring long term benefits, if your reputation within the organisation is to be preserved.

What other pressures are there facing the internal consultant? These may be many:

- time: if you are a scarce resource, and if you establish a good reputation throughout the organisation, you may win more client work than you can cope with.
- role conflict: this may be a particular problem if you combine your consulting role with line management responsibility. Your consult-

ing work may suffer if you have to devote a considerable proportion of your time to day-to-day management.

- being 'leaned on' by individual managers to do work for them when you have other priorities.
- becoming a 'dumping ground' for all kinds of work that is not, strictly speaking, part of your consulting role. Again, this can happen all too easily if you become recognised as a sound source of advice throughout the organisation.
- some managers can be highly territorial and are simply unwilling to release control of a project to someone who is not directly under their responsibility. They may tend to belittle your role and declare that they consider you not expert enough in their area of specialism. This may result in parts of the organisation being 'off limits' for you.
- you may find it difficult to acquire the necessary resources to do your job properly. For instance, it can be very difficult indeed to have staff seconded away from their own departments to work on project teams.
- you may find it difficult to justify your existence, particularly if you are set utilisation targets that you cannot meet and are therefore spending a significant part of your time without client work.

Responding to these pressures requires the development of attitudes that may be new and unfamiliar, particularly if your previous
experience has been in a line management role. In many ways, it is
easier for a line manager to become an external consultant than an
internal consultant. If you join one of the major professional consulting firms, for example, you are surrounded by other, more
experienced consultants and the support processes are in place to
ease you into your new role. This is unlikely to be the case if you are
setting up an internal consulting practice. Specifically, then, what
attitudes are required?

Adopting a professional consulting approach

This means a number of things: predominantly being proactive in
acquiring all the technical skills necessary to carry out your work.

Consulting skills, such as client and project management and effective presentation techniques, are covered in this book. Training courses are available which provide coaching in the key skills and techniques, and use role play exercises to reinforce these. You might also usefully make contact with other consultants (even external ones!) who in many cases will be happy to give you support and advice concerning specific aspects of the role.

It is also important that as a consultant you regard other people in the organisation as clients first and foremost, rather than simply as colleagues. This does not mean you should treat them differently in your day-to-day relations; however, you should be aware of the need to present a professional image at all times, and that the nature of your role means that you are effectively independent from them. Remember, there may come a time when you are charging them fees for your services.

Selling yourself positively

You will need to take positive steps to ensure you are known throughout the organisation, and are regarded as a person who can help managers overcome their problems. This is particularly important in the early stages, and if you are new to the organisation. Beware, however, of going 'over the top' on publicity seeking if you don't win work immediately. Building a presence can take time, and you may have to be patient in developing relationships with potential clients.

Being diplomatic . . . but firm

You may need to be diplomatic with some managers, but don't be swayed into agreeing with them for the sake of being agreeable. Ultimately, the worst thing you can do is embark on a project that fails to address the real needs of the client and of the organisation as a whole. In some cases you may need to tell people that they are not focused in the right direction, and that their needs are other than they perceive them to be.

Being flexible

As a consultant, you may sometimes be working on your own, sometimes as part of a team. You may not always know the other team members well, and may have to take on trust their skills, attitudes and commitment. You will not be working in an ordered hierarchy. This calls for a degree of flexibility not normally required of line managers. At one level, it involves being prepared to help other team members when they get into difficulties. At another level it means having the confidence of your convictions, even when there is opposition or little support for your proposals.

'Thinking process consulting'

As stated above, you can't run away from the results of your projects in the way an external consultant often can. You need, therefore, to involve your clients closely in your work, gaining commitment from them as the project progresses. It is very important not to become detached from your clients, so that they have the opportunity of distancing themselves from tough decisions concerning implementation.

Understanding the business

One of your key competitive advantages over external consultants is your knowledge of the culture and objectives of the organisation in which you work. Make sure, therefore, that you do thoroughly know your business. If you don't, you will rapidly lose credibility and, more seriously, may simply give your clients poor advice.

If you are to achieve status within the organisation, you need at an early stage to define clearly your role and responsibilities. One of the best ways of doing this is to draw up a job description, setting out your main tasks and objectives and the knowledge, skills and experience you require to carry out your job properly. Clearly, the detail of this will vary according to the circumstances; however, an example of a 'generic' job description for an internal consultant is set out in Fig. 2.1 for illustrative purposes.

JOB PROFILE

Job title: Management Consultant

Reporting to: Head of Internal Consulting Unit

Key Objectives

To identify problems and issues associated with the development of our business. To analyse thoroughly the needs of managers and work with them as clients to develop solutions to their business problems. To help with the implementation of new business solutions.

Major responsibilities

- to identify opportunities to improve the company's business performance,
- to develop relationships with managers and staff throughout the organisation, and become recognised as a source of support,
- to prepare proposals to help managers identify and implement business solutions,
- to undertake projects, working with clients to develop these solutions and meet their business needs,
- to manage staff seconded to project teams, ensuring their work is carried out to high quality standards and within budget,
- to assist managers with implementation of agreed recommendations,
- to assist the Head of the Internal Consulting Unit in the marketing and promotion of the Unit.

Skills, qualifications and experience required

Degree level education (preferably in a business discipline). Postgraduate qualification in a management subject preferred. A minimum of five years' line experience, with at least one year in a management role. Extensive knowledge of the company including its organisation, culture and business objectives. Project management experience desirable. Good presentation, analytical and interpersonal skills essential.

Key internal/external relationships

Regular contact with the Head of the Internal Consulting Unit. Day-to-day contact with clients and staff seconded onto project teams. Relationships with external contacts (e.g. sources of information in other companies, suppliers of services).

Fig. 2.1 Generic job description for an internal consultant.

BUILDING A PRESENCE AS AN INTERNAL CONSULTANT

Imagine you are a newly-established internal consultant, working in a large and diverse organisation as a facilitator of change management. You may be part of a consulting team, an independent unit with no direct line reporting to operational or other support functions. Alternatively, you may be combining your consulting role with some line management responsibilities. Either way, there will be a need to establish your credibility throughout the organisation, so that potential clients know of your existence and wish to make use of your expertise. From this will come the leads that ultimately progress to 'won work'. Building a presence calls for a range of skills related to making contact with people and the identification of client needs and opportunities.

Networking

Networking is an absolutely essential skill for the internal consultant. It requires a proactive approach, involving continual contact with managers throughout the organisation, to become known as an internal resource, establish credibility and tap into the opportunities and resources they can provide.

Networking opportunities can come in many ways:

- calling on managers in their offices (with or without a prior appointment) to make initial contact and describe your role and objectives. This is particularly appropriate for a newly-appointed consultant, who will have a need to build a profile quickly and where there may be an interest on the part of potential clients to find out what he or she is like.
- informal contacts made during corporate events such as training courses or conferences. Rapport built up with colleagues at such events can be very valuable as further contact in the work context takes place.
- chance encounters (in the corridor or the staff restaurant) can often be the launchpad to a more formal presentation. Such

encounters should be followed up, either through a meeting or by telephone.

- telephone calls themselves can be turned around into valuable introductions. 'Cold-calling' is to be discouraged (usually it is better to go and visit the contact in person) but where the person is calling you there may be an opportunity to introduce yourself and perhaps set up a future meeting to discuss issues in more detail.

- sometimes the opportunity is given to make a formal presentation, either to a small working group or a wider audience such as conference delegates. This can be an excellent means of introduction to people in the organisation of all levels and different disciplines.

'Becoming known' will involve knocking on doors, but not in such a way as to appear over-anxious to win work or to sell services that are irrelevant or inappropriate. It is impossible to be didactic about the best approach to take, as this will depend on the personality of the consultant and the attitudes and expectations of contacts. It is clearly important to know as much as possible about your contacts before going to visit them; some may welcome an unannounced face round the door, whereas others may regard it as a thoroughly unwelcome intrusion! If in doubt, play safe, the initial contact is likely to be of paramount importance in determining the basis of any future relationship.

However, a number of basic principles in networking can be clearly stated:

- when introducing yourself, stick as closely as possible to a well-rehearsed story. It is important not to give widely differing messages to different people in the same organisation.

- it is equally important not to take too long in describing your experience and abilities. The people you will be dealing with may be busy and will not be interested in an exhaustive list of your past achievements. Alternatively, spend a little time describing the **benefits** your consulting approach can bring. This will be of much more interest.

- establish confidence in yourself. This can be done in many ways, for example by following up quickly on enquiries, demonstrating that you know what you are talking about and can relate to the problems and issues being faced. Try as far as possible to educate and inform people throughout the organisation. In particular, be proactive in bringing to their attention issues of importance you believe they may be unaware of.

A further key element of networking is the ability to listen and learn. Contacts with colleagues elsewhere in the organisation should be regarded as your prime source of information about the role and objectives of their own departments or work units and the problems, conflicts and issues being faced. Remember it is your wide-ranging knowledge and understanding of the organisation that is to be one of your key competitive advantages. Your information must therefore be broad, relevant and up to date, and must encompass both hard data and 'soft' issues such as the attitudes of key managers, the culture of the organisation and staff morale. You should develop the habit of writing a brief file note, for your own use, following any contact which leads to information being obtained; otherwise there is the likelihood that the context will be lost.

In addition to providing information, colleagues with whom you have established good contacts can be of help in a number of other ways. They can identify opportunities for consulting work – either in their own units or elsewhere – and can identify and introduce other people in the organisation who are influential or may be potential project sponsors. There may also be the opportunity to involve them in consulting projects, either by seconding them to the project team or having them provide *ad hoc* support and advice, contributing their own particular experience or expertise to achieve better results.

Setting up an internal consulting office

Establishing a consulting office may seem an obvious task for a newly-appointed consultant, but it should not be taken lightly. It is important that your office reinforces your professional image, and at the same time is set up in such a way as to differentiate you from line functions within the organisation.

To a large extent this can be achieved by the actual location and physical layout of your office. Factors that you need to bear in mind are:

- visibility: your office should not be buried away at a remote location, or in some corner of the main office building which is rarely visited by staff. Nor should it be located in the middle of some line function or department, where you will be associated with the work of that department rather than regarded as an independent source of advice. Ideally you need to be in a situation where people of all levels and backgrounds walk past your front door – not next to the staff restaurant, but not sharing the dizzy heights of the top executives' suite either! People need to know you are there, and not be afraid to walk in and talk to you. Even when you are highly visible, it will pay for you to advertise your whereabouts as widely as possible. Make sure your office is properly signposted, that there is a prominent nameplate on the front door. Make sure you are recorded as a separate entry in the internal telephone directory, and on lists of departments displayed in lifts, entrance halls and lobbies.
- creating an atmosphere conducive to good client relations. You will need to be able to talk to people confidentially on many occasions, so if your main workspace is not enclosed you will need a separate enclosed space, such as an interview room, in close proximity and readily available. The setup of the room where you conduct meetings and interviews should be relaxed and informal. The nature of your job means that most discussions will be better conducted around a coffee-table rather than more formally across a desk. You should keep your office tidy at all times. Not only will this create a better impression, but you should not get into the habit of leaving 'client' papers and documents lying around. They may be sensitive to the client concerned, or confidential.
- the furnishing and decor of your office can also be important in creating the right image. If possible, try to obtain furniture different from the standard issue throughout the organisation, as this will help to differentiate you from line departments. Beware, however, of ordering furniture that is obviously more opulent and expensive than that in place elsewhere, as the last thing you want is

to create an 'elitist' image. This applies equally to decorative items and office paraphernalia such as pictures, plants, coffee percolators, etc. Your overall aim should be to create a relaxed, open environment in your office, distinctive without being exclusive.

When setting up your office you need to establish the level of support facilities you will be allocated. Secretarial and administrative support is particularly important. If you are a 'sole practitioner', and you are able to use WP and other software packages, you may not need a full-time secretary or office administrator. However, you will certainly need **some** support, and where this is shared or borrowed from another function you must establish the availability of your administrator, and that he/she has the skills required to help you in your job. Think also about the technology you will need. At the very least, this is likely to include a PC with word processing, spreadsheet modelling and graphics packages, and probably some administrative system to facilitate budget control, client billing and expenses.

Another important area for you to consider is the 'clout' you will have in obtaining the services of staff elsewhere in the organisation for secondment onto project teams. This is a key issue where you are working on your own or in a small team of consultants, and where you will frequently have to make up project teams from staff not directly within your responsibility. Not surprisingly, the people you are most likely to want are usually those whom line managers are most reluctant to release. You need to know if you will be supported by senior management when you put in requests for staff secondments.

This raises the whole issue of identifying your allies and supporters throughout the organisation. A fine balance is required here. On one hand you clearly need the support of top management – particularly in the early stages – but it can be dangerous to be associated too closely with just one or two senior people. Not only are you vulnerable if they leave the organisation or fall out of favour, but if they are heavy-handed (for instance, in meeting your needs at the expense of other people's) they can create general hostility towards you and what you are trying to achieve. Ideally, you want to create a broad base of support which enables you to obtain the resources you need without upsetting too many people.

Marketing your services

Marketing is an activity you will need to undertake from the beginning of your consulting career, and sustain strongly if you are to maintain interest in your services amongst potential clients. There are many lessons to be learned from external consultants here, although it is important not to get carried away as external consultants sometimes do, and bore your target audience to death. Effective ways of carrying out marketing include:

- events such as presentations, workshops and 'business breakfasts';
- targeting specific clients,
- distributing experience summary sheets and other printed material;
- publicising your successes and achievements.

Marketing events

Only you will know what type of event is most appropriate. This will depend largely on two factors: first, the culture within the organisation; the attitudes of managers and, critically, their attention span; second, the type of message you want to put across. Above all, you should not consider launching an event of any kind until you have decided on a theme or message that you believe will be of interest to your intended audience. The message could be highly general ('Hello, here I am, this is what I can do for you') or highly specific (In response to the company's current cashflow problems, we have developed a new approach to budgeting that we want to tell you about . . .'). The type of message will be instrumental in determining the main features of the event: what structure, when and where to hold it, who to invite and what steps to take afterwards.

- **what structure:** a prime objective of any event should be to put invitees at their ease, and therefore in a better frame of mind to a) express their views freely, and b) feel well-disposed towards you (and hopefully, ultimately make use of your services). Avoid going on too long, and above all don't lecture your audience. Most events involve a brief formal presentation by the consultant, followed by open discussion. Usually this works quite well, although you may need to think of some prompts to get the discussion going if the audience is reserved. Any presentation should not be too complicated; you should aim to put across a simple message and then generate a discussion lasting no more than half an hour. Overhead slides are the most commonly used presentation aid.

- **when:** in the evening, if you can be sure your audience will stay to listen to you. If not, you should hold the event during work time or over a lunch period (providing a buffet for delegates in the latter case). Business breakfasts tend to be associated with the power culture of the 1980s and are probably best avoided.

- **where:** hiring a room in a hotel or other conveniently situated external venue is best in most cases. This creates more interest among the delegates, and can help to differentiate you. If an internal venue is necessary, try to arrange it so that interruptions are kept to a minimum.

- **whom to invite:** if your theme is very specific and likely to be of interest to a narrow range of people, individual invitations are more appropriate. Where the theme is wider it is likely to be better to issue an open invitation. If there are certain managers you would particularly like to be there, follow up any written invitation with a phone call.

- **afterwards:** issue people who have attended with an information pack (this may include any presentation slides you have used, plus **brief** written information likely to be of interest). Immediately after the event you should sit down and take stock of the audience response, thinking particularly of areas of most general interest, and any people who have indicated specific interests. You will then be in a better position to follow these up later. It can be helpful to have a colleague with you at an event, both to share the present-ation and give feedback afterwards on delegate response.

Targeting specific clients

There may be several reasons why a particular person within the organisation should be a 'target client':

- they are well disposed towards you. If you are networking

effectively, you should certainly get a good feel for those people in the organisation who are your supporters, and those who are not. Your supporters are more likely to commission projects and – assuming there is something you can genuinely help them with – you should therefore target them vigorously. Beware, however, of selling something your client doesn't need, just because they are easy to sell to. Giving them something they don't want can make an enemy of a supporter!

- you have identified that they have a particular need you can meet. Even if they are not well-disposed towards you (or are at best neutral) you must establish contact with them to explain your ideas and sell the benefits of your approach.
- if you specialise in a particular functional area, such as IT, marketing or human resources management, your main target clients will be in the service departments responsible for these functions. Remember however, that services have their users who may just as legitimately become your targets (for example, you may see an opportunity to improve use of IT in a specific business area, reviewing needs from a business point of view).

Having identified your targets, what approaches should you adopt? Clearly, you should not begin an approach until you have something convincing to say: this might be a particular idea you have had, something you wish to bring to their attention or to demonstrate. It may be a good idea, from time to time, to mail them something – perhaps a magazine article or a brochure. In some circumstances it may be appropriate to make an approach through a third party, for instance a 'supporter' in the organisation who knows them better than you do, and who can introduce you. The most important thing is to think through your approach and, taking account of what you have to offer and your understanding of the person concerned, adapt your approach accordingly.

If it is important to make the right initial approach, it is equally important to maintain the contact when it has been established. This does not mean bombarding your target with information or making a nuisance of yourself; but as a rule of thumb you should aim to make some kind of contact, however slight, at least once every two to three weeks. You must ensure that you are in the person's mind, should the opportunity to do a piece of work for them come along.

Experience summary sheets and other material

Many consultants prepare lengthy CVs which are issued to clients, usually attached to formal proposals to carry out work. In the internal consulting context, it is more appropriate to produce shorter, punchier summaries of experience and qualifications which can be sent to potential clients or given to them by hand. Such summaries will have more immediate impact and are likely to create the impression that you are keen to become known and help managers solve their problems.

An example of an experience summary is set out in Fig. 2.2. As can be seen, it 'introduces' the consultant concerned and contains short, punchy statements of her skills and work experience. It also includes a photograph – a useful means both of attracting the reader's interest and facilitating easy recognition. Crucially, it sets out how the consultant can help in solving management problems, and includes a contact number. Avoid the temptation to stretch the experience summary beyond a single A4 page; this will considerably reduce it's impact and the likelihood of it being read. If your experience is too wide-ranging to be incorporated onto one page, prepare two, or at most three different versions to be issued according to different circumstances.

Production of a printed brochure can be a valuable marketing tool to publicise a multi-disciplinary consultancy or where a number of consultants work together in a unit. The objective here is to promote the services of the unit as a whole, rather than an individual. Brochures should be professionally printed, in the company's 'house style' but ideally with some differentiating feature such as use of a logo or distinctive colour. A 'foldover' format, of half A4 size and with no more than two or three double sides should be sufficient to incorporate all the information you need to convey. This might include:

● the background or 'history' of the consulting unit;
● the range of services offered;

HUMAN RESOURCE MANAGEMENT AND POLICY

Practical and professional advice across the broad spectrum of human resource issues including:

- Contracts of Employment
- Employee Benefits
- Sickness and Absence Control
- Employee Communication and Participation
- Employment Law
- Discipline and Grievance Procedures
- Redundancy and Redeployment
- Design and Implementation of
  Personnel Records Systems
- Staff Welfare
- Negotiating Terms and Conditions
- Expatriate Management

CLAUDINE GERNON
AGE 33
CONSULTANT

Previous Experience
Northwickshire
Building Society

Specialism
Considerable experience encompassing the full range of personnel management systems and techniques. This has been in the fields of policy development and senior management advice as well as in application and control.

Clients who have used these services include:
- EUROPEAN PRODUCTION DIVISION
  Design of a pan-European computerised staff records system
- CENTRAL ACCOUNTING DEPARTMENT
  Development and delivery of a staff communications programme
- Contact: Internal Consulting Unit × 4833

BENEFITS TO CLIENTS
- Ensuring personnel systems support the achievement of business objectives
- Maintaining control of the human resource
- Fostering good employee relations to the benefit of the business and staff alike
- Avoiding damaging internal disputes and external investigations

Fig. 2.2 Sample experience summary sheet

- how these services can be of benefit, both to individuals and the business as a whole;
- the qualifications and expertise of the unit (ideally including one or two examples of successful projects);
- the names and brief bio-details of the consultants (with photographs if possible);
- who to contact for further information. This is likely to be the head of the consulting unit.

How should experience summaries and brochures be used to help build up a presence? This depends very much on the structure and objectives of the organisation, the role of the consultants within it, and the attitudes of senior managers. An initial 'mailshot' should be sufficiently widespread to generate broad recognition, without flooding the organisation completely. In most circumstances, it should probably be limited to department heads plus any other managers who are known or likely to have an interest in the services being offered. A stock should be retained so that copies can be given to people who have raised specific enquiries or as further contacts are established. The text should be modified as further consulting experience within the organisation is gained, possibly leading to re-issue at a future date when the content has changed significantly from the original version.

Publicising your successes and achievements

Nothing impresses people more than a publication, an appearance on radio, TV or at a conference, or an interview with you in a newspaper or magazine. Many people are completely overawed when colleagues of theirs achieve some sort of minor fame; but despite this, it is not as difficult as most people think to win an opportunity to speak at a conference or publish an article. This is something you may be able to make use of in building your presence as an internal consultant. If you have an idea that you think may be of interest, therefore, seek out opportunities to publicise it. Many professional and trade magazines are more than willing to accept articles for publication (though don't expect payment for them). Often a phone call to the editor explaining your idea is enough to gain acceptance. Equally, it is often quite easy to win a platform slot at a seminar or conference, particularly if you have some specialist experience and represent a 'blue chip' organisation. Circulate copies of your article, presentation synopsis or overhead slides as soon as possible to people within the organisation who are likely to be interested. Make sure that a report appears in the in-house magazine. Above all, use your new-found fame to build your standing in the organisation as a professional person whose ideas are respected and widely sought.

Make use also, of anything in your background or personal interests that will help to distinguish you and make you appear impressive to your potential clients. For example:

- academic achievements: if you have a double first from Cambridge, or an MBA from INSEAD, make sure people get to know this. It goes without saying that your academic and professional qualifications should be stated in your publicity material.
- previous service with blue chip companies (sound private sector experience goes down particularly well in the public sector).
- links with professional associations, particularly any offices you have held at local or national level. Commitments to charities, local government or community service bodies, part-time lecturing activities or school governorships can all be worth publicising, although be careful if these are likely to be controversial or single you out as an 'activist'.
- links with well-known or professionally respected people such as academics, business people or political figures can add to your standing if used carefully.
- any previous books or articles published or public appearances you have made can be worth publicising, particularly if the subject matter is relevant to your work or they achieved special notice and acclaim at the time.

It may appear cynical to some people to mention some of these things in the context of publicity-seeking. However, we stop short of suggesting you should develop personal interests or become involved in activities purely for the purpose of generating publicity for your work. Many external consultants, and business people in other walks of life, **are** encouraged to do this by their employers.

Getting to know your organisation

We have referred earlier to the need for the internal consultant to understand the organisation of which he/she is a part, in order to gain credibility and competitive advantage. What exactly does this mean, and how does the consultant go about acquiring the necessary knowledge?

Essentially, 'getting to know your organisation' is a process of absorption in which your understanding will deepen and evolve as long as you work there. However there is a need to acquire a good deal of base information as quickly as possible. This will encompass:

- the history and background of the organisation;
- the overall mission and associated business objectives;
- the beliefs and attitudes of the Directors and top management;
- the beliefs, attitudes and skills of the staff;
- the culture of the organisation;
- markets and market threats/opportunities;
- competitor positioning;
- owner/shareholder views.

Your sources of information on these and other issues may be many and varied, coming from both inside the organisation and without. Networking within the organisation will enable you to talk to a lot of people and obtain a wide range of facts, opinions and attitudes. You should also take the trouble to obtain and read as much written material as possible, including annual report and accounts, special reports, correspondence, company histories, in-house magazines; in short, anything you can lay your hands on that can add to your knowledge or understanding. You should try and obtain records and statistics covering as many areas of activity as possible. Above all, you should **observe** the organisational environment. How do people behave in their interpersonal relationships? What are the 'war stories' and jokes that the organisation tells about itself? Which managers are respected, reviled, revered? Apart from behaviour, every organisation has its icons and symbols: the company car, allocation of offices, even the houseplants or the style of nameplates on managers' doors. These too will tell you a good deal about the culture of the organisation, how it regards itself and the people who work within it.

External information can be equally important, not least because you may learn things about the organisation that few other people within it know. You should obtain transcripts of any articles on the organisation that appear in newspapers and magazines. You should talk extensively to suppliers, customers, counterparts or managers in competitor organisations. Above all, you should aim to find out what the outside world **thinks** about your organisation, and as much as possible about its position in the market and/or social environment.

This emphasis on gaining information may seem like overkill, but it will be critical to achieving the status you require to carry out your role effectively. You need at once to become integrated within the organisation, while having sufficiently wide-ranging and detached information to be able to identify and comment on issues that may not be apparent to people who are buried within their line management roles.

Setting yourself goals

Setting targets and goals for yourself is never easy, particularly when you are still becoming established in your role. Nevertheless, it is important to do this from the outset, if only to give yourself some benchmarks against which to measure your success.

External consultants are typically set goals on an annual basis, subject to review at regular intervals during the year. Frequently, these include:

- generating a certain number of leads during the year. A 'lead' is usually defined as a specific enquiry from a prospective client that leads directly to the submission of a proposal.
- winning a specified number of projects, or a certain level of fee-earning work. In the context of external consulting, it is not always easy to determine who has actually 'won' a piece of work, as a team of consultants may have been involved in writing the proposal,

making presentations or otherwise persuading the client to go ahead (in some cases this leads to the same piece of work being claimed as a win by several different consultants). For an internal consultant it should, in most cases, be easier to identify the person primarily responsible.

- spending a certain percentage of total work time on fee-earning client work. Usually referred to as 'utilisation', this is the key measure for many external consultants as it broadly reflects their market value: good consultants get put on jobs, bad ones don't.
- training: acquiring or improving a particular technical skill such as report writing, effective presentations or selling skills.
- developing detailed knowledge of an industry sector, a functional area or management technique (e.g. total quality, IT project management).
- developing and delivering marketing activities such as a presentation, survey or conference.

Depending on the specific circumstances, any of these goals can be appropriate for the internal consultant. You should probably set yourself no more than four to six individual targets initially, and should review your progress carefully throughout the year. If it becomes clear over time that a specific target is unattainable, either due to factors beyond your control or because you overestimated your capabilities, you should make adjustments accordingly. There is no point in setting targets that you can't achieve, or conversely that are so easy to achieve that they are unchallenging.

Doing external consulting work

It is not unusual for successful internal consulting practices to diversify by doing projects for clients other than their parent organisation. A good example is CIE Consult, the consulting unit of the Irish Railways company, which carries out work for other railway and engineering companies throughout the world (when we last had dealings with them, they were bidding for a major reconstruction study for the Syrian railway company).

Winning and carrying out external projects can add variety and interest to the work of the internal consultant, engendering a broader view and the development of greater commercial and interpersonal skills. However, for most internal consultancies it should be regarded as a complementary rather than a mainstream activity, that should only be considered when they have established a good reputation and sound professional practices.

There are a certain number of practical considerations to be observed in commencing external consulting work:

- you cannot hope to cover as broad a spectrum as the major consulting practices. Because of your size and the fact that your main client (i.e. your parent organisation) is industry specific, you will have neither the resources nor the credibility to give advice across sectors. You should aim, therefore, to build on one of your key strengths – your detailed knowledge of your industry and/or functional specialism. The CIE Consult example is a good one to follow here; it has established a good reputation for engineering consultancy and has in the main targeted Third World railway organisations where major development projects are regularly sponsored by bodies such as the World Bank and the European Bank for Reconstruction and Development.
- you must have sufficient resources to carry out work won, while not neglecting the needs of your own organisation. If you are a 'sole practitioner', you may find it difficult to do external work. If you are part of a small practice of, perhaps, five consultants or more, there may be more time to devote to externally focused marketing and project work.
- beware of problems concerning ethics/confidentiality. If you are industry specific your potential clients may also be your competitors, either immediately or in the longer term. You don't want to give away your own organisation's business secrets, or waste any competitive advantage you have gained for it through the benefits of your internal consultancy work.
- building a name for yourself will largely come from the quality of the work you do for your own organisation. It is likely that a high proportion of your leads will come by word of mouth, as managers from your organisation talk to their counterparts in other com-

panies. However, you will need to carry out extensive marketing activities to build up your practice. These will include many of the activities already outlined in this chapter, but may also include: setting up stands at conferences/business fairs; advertising in trade or other journals; targeting and establishing contact directly with potential clients; registering with development banks or other sponsors that fund development projects.

- your fee structure is something you will need to consider carefully. You cannot expect to charge clients the sort of rates charged by major consulting firms, yet on the other hand you don't want to pitch yourself so low as to appear desperate to win work. A lot depends on your internal pricing structure and cost base. External fees can be a very useful way of offsetting internal costs if you operate as a cost centre rather than a profit centre.

- it can be highly beneficial to form strategic alliances with other consultancies or organisations, particularly for large-scale projects. If you have established a good reputation in a specialist field, you can be a very attractive partner, for example, to a major consultancy bidding for a big overseas contract. Although the major consultancy may have excellent all-round consulting skills and good theoretical knowledge of an industry's problems and issues, your **practical** understanding of these issues can be very important to clients and may be instrumental in winning the work. In forming any alliance, it is obviously important to establish at the outset the project management arrangements including the way the work will be split, the roles and responsibilities of yourself/your own consultants and the fee structure. When the work begins, adaptability is all-important; you will be working with people you do not know, consulting styles and standards may be different, and you will need to establish yourself as a good team player if you are to win respect (and with it, hopefully, the opportunity for further work in future).

However professional you are in your approach, be prepared for competition not only from the major consultancies but also smaller 'niche' consultancies such as your own. They are likely to have practical sector or technical knowledge comparable with your own, their fees will be closer to yours and they may be more attuned to selling themselves professionally. You are likely to experience many disappointments, losing projects that you thought you had won or that you **should** have won. But despite these disappointments, be positive; if you have a 'unique selling point' and the resources to make use of this in the external consulting context, there is no reason why you should not succeed.

3

EFFICIENT FACT-FINDING AND INFORMATION ANALYSIS

In this chapter we consider the 'core' consulting skills in the area of fact-finding and analysis. These include:

- how to establish clearly agreed terms of reference, and set up a project;
- defining the difference between the client and the sponsor;
- interviewing skills in the consulting context;
- developing and mounting effective surveys; and
- checking and analysing information.

PROJECT SETUP

You are now becoming established as an internal consultant. You have built a presence within the organisation, have met a wide range of managers and staff and made them aware of your skills and experience. You receive your first enquiry; your first opportunity to carry out a piece of consulting work. How do you respond?

Initial client contact

Your first task is to establish the exact nature of the enquiry, and whether or not it is a genuine opportunity. This will inevitably require a meeting with the instigator of the enquiry, who may or may not be the sponsor. The main purposes of the initial meeting should be:

- to establish the nature of the work required, whether indeed it represents a genuine client **need**, and whether it is a piece of work that you can actually carry out; and
- to identify the project sponsor and any other key people who can approve the work or influence the decision to go ahead.

Following the initial contact, there may be many reasons why you should decide not to go ahead. It may be that you cannot agree with the client that the work is actually needed or is possible to achieve. Many potential clients come with a 'wish list' that either far exceeds achievable reality, or is at odds with other initiatives taking place within the organisation. In this circumstance, to go ahead with the work could be potentially damaging, even if the project itself were successful in a narrow sense. It may be that you do not have the skills to carry out the work, and are not able to call upon other resources from within the organisation to do it. A further reason for not taking things further may simply be that you are not convinced that your contact has any authority to commission the work.

It is important to distinguish at an early stage between the project sponsor and the client where they are not the same, because they have different objectives and need therefore to be treated in different ways. Frequently, the client will be looking for as much advice and support as they can get, irrespective of the costs or other resource implications. The sponsor on the other hand will be looking for value for money, and is likely to want to monitor closely the progress made in a particular project against agreed budgets. In this context:

- **the client** is the recipient of the consulting services being provided, who will ultimately receive the benefits of the work carried out and with whom there must be close co-operation throughout the project.
- **the sponsor** is the person or institution that commissions, and pays for, the work being done. In some cases, client and sponsor are one and the same; however this is not necessarily the case. For example, much of the work carried out by UK consulting firms for Third World governments and organisations (the client) is funded by independent institutions (the sponsor) such as the World Bank and the Overseas Development Administration (ODA). In the

internal consulting context, a project where the beneficiary is a particular function or working group may be sponsored separately by, for example, the Board, the Chief Executive or an internal research and development group.

Equally, it is important to be able to determine that both the client and sponsor are really committed to commissioning a consultant to go ahead. If either is uncommitted, there are likely to be severe problems. This situation is not as uncommon as might be expected; for example, client staff frequently feel threatened by change that is proposed from above, and can be highly resistant to a project they suspect may affect them adversely.

The checklist set out in Table 3.1 indicates some of the questions a consultant may need to consider in ascertaining the objectives of, respectively, client and sponsor, and whether there is likely to be conflict between them.

If, for whatever reason, you are unwilling to proceed with a project, it is best to tell your contact as soon as possible, giving your reasons. In most cases this is likely to enhance rather than damage your credibility, particularly if you are able to offer an alternative solution or can redirect the contact in a more appropriate direction. It is even possible that you may be able to create a consulting opportunity in a different direction – for example, if you can convince your contact that his needs are different from those he originally imagined.

Developing things further

However, assuming you have established some common ground with your contact at the initial meeting and there is some intention on both sides to proceed, a lot of information may need to be obtained before you can submit a full proposal. Remember, you should aim to prepare a project proposal setting out the terms of reference, even if the outcome of your initial meeting has been an agreement to go ahead. It is essential to have full understanding between consultant and client regarding the exact nature of the work to be done, the deliverables, the time and other resources required and, of course, the costs.

Table 3.1 Checklist of essential points before committing to project

Question: relates to...	The Client	The Sponsor
Who initiated the enquiry?	x	x
Does the sponsor have authority to commission the work?		x
What are the sponsor's needs?		x
What are the client's needs?	x	
Do the client and sponsor recognise these needs?	x	x
Who are the key client personnel involved?	x	
Will these personnel support the project?	x	
What is the relationship between sponsor and client?	x	x
Do any conflicts of interest exist?	x	x
Has the client properly identified issues and critical success factors?	x	
How does the work fit in with overall business strategy?	x	x
Do the client and sponsor have a realistic perception of the scope of the work required?	x	x

This information-gathering should take the form of a preliminary survey covering all information areas necessary both to put together the proposal and begin the project 'from a running start'. It should therefore include:

- factual information concerning the organisation that is needed to carry out the project work. Frequently this will include detailed and sensitive information concerning specific departments or work areas, such as the current organisation of work, performance measures and work objectives, budgets, skills, use of technology, and reputation throughout the organisation. It may also include the backgrounds and attitudes of key staff.

- information concerning the resources you will require to carry out the project, particularly the composition of the project team. In many cases you will need either the technical input of staff with particular skills or experience relevant to the work, or support staff to carry out administrative tasks or research. You need to know a) whether such staff are to be found within the organisation, and b) the extent of their availability to the project team.

- knowledge of the client: what does he/she expect in terms of deliverables and benefits? How does the work fit in with other aspects of his/her strategy? What are the critical success factors, and what will be the working relationship with the consultant throughout the project?

- understanding of how the work fits into the 'big picture': i.e. the future impact of the work on the organisation as a whole, any other interested parties who should be informed or involved, any potential overlaps or conflicts of interest.

Some items of information should be easy to obtain, through further meetings with the client or access to readily obtainable reports and documents – others may be more difficult. It may be necessary to approach other colleagues not directly involved in the project to ascertain their views, or to gain access to sensitive information concerning, for instance, departmental or individual performance. There may also be the need to negotiate with managers concerning the release of key staff for secondment onto the project team.

Initial workplan

Having obtained all necessary preliminary information, the logical next step before preparing the proposal is to prepare a project workplan. Essentially, this is your initial estimate of the direction the project will take, the number of distinct phases required and the amount of time and resources required to take the work to completion.

External consultants, who will probably have carried out similar projects elsewhere and who therefore have previous experience of the problems and issues encountered, are likely to be better placed to draw up an accurate project workplan than an internal consultant with much more limited experience in this respect. However, it is important to bear in mind that the workplan presents no more than a broad outline of the project, and that the details will inevitably need some modification as the work progresses. Even the most meticulous of external consulting firms, making use of project management computer packages to facilitate the process, draw up workplans that in the end prove to be hugely wide of the mark in terms of the actual resources required. In our experience, it is better at this stage to stick to a fairly simple model rather than try to make use of sophisticated computer software as an 'aid' to project management.

A project workplan is essentially a matrix that takes account of the following factors:

- the project phases: i.e. the successive stages to the project, including any interim progress report meetings or management workshops to develop findings and ideas.
- project deliverables: in addition to the final deliverables, any interim reports or discussion documents presented during the project.
- the actual time estimated to be required for the project, measured in man-hours or man-days and taking account of all consultants or other staff involved. It is typical for external consultants to build in an additional contingency, often of around 10 per cent, to take account of project management and 'unexpected' occurrences.
- the elapsed time estimated to be required: i.e. the number of weeks or months necessary to take the project from beginning to end, taking account of consultant availability, limitations on access to key staff or other likely constraints.
- consultant costs: usually this is a simple multiplication between the consultants' hourly fee rates and the estimated number of hours required. It does not necessarily reflect the costs that will be charged to the client, as this may be on a basis other than 'standard rates'. Whatever the charging arrangement is to be, it is essential to

go through this exercise as it gives an accurate estimate of the
actual costs involved.

● other expenses: these may include estimates of travelling costs and
overnight accommodation, report production, secretarial support
and the cost of any equipment, materials or publications required.
Again, it is common to build in a contingency' of ten to fifteen per
cent to cater for any unexpected additional costs.

Set out below are examples of the type of project planning pro
formas used by external consulting firms in order to prepare proposals. It is standard practice for these pro formas to be completed by
the project manager, usually by hand. As can be seen there are three
separate forms, entitled 'Project Plan', 'Project Budget', and 'Project
Expense Budget'. The examples shown have been completed for an
imaginary project, entitled 'Preparation of Job Descriptions for the
Production Staff of the Stonyshire Manufacturing Company'.

A brief description of this imaginary project plan is set out in Fig.
3.1.

Project plan

The project has been planned to take place over three phases: an
initial phase in which the main task is a series of interviews with
managers and staff, a second phase involving the preparation of
written job descriptions and their verification, and a brief third phase
in which a report will be prepared incorporating the finalised descriptions. Each phase is represented by a block on the engagement plan,
showing the amount of elapsed time estimated for each. Interim and
final meetings with the client are represented as triangles on the plan.

Project budget

Against each of the three phases, Fig. 3.2 this shows the amount of
estimated time required by each of the three staff engaged for the
project. These staff are the project manager (i.e. the consultant who
prepared the workplan and who will lead the engagement) and two
job analysts (staff seconded from the personnel department who will

PROJECT PLAN

Client ....Production Division....

Project title ....Preparation of Job Descriptions....

Project No. ....0041....

WORK AREA	Consultant	\<--- Weeks ---\>										Man Days
		1	2	3	4	5	6	7	8	9	10	
PHASE I Initial meeting	MB	◄										0·5
Draw up job description form	MB	▦										0·5
Job holders interviews	LC/JS		▦	▦	▦							12
Department Head interviews	MB/LC/JS			▦								3
Progress meeting	MB					◄						1
PHASE II Job description preparation	MB/LC/JS						▦	▦				5
Further Department Head interviews	MB/LC/JS								▦			3
PHASE III Progress meeting	MB									◄		1
Revision of job descriptions	MB/LC/JS									▦		2
Final meeting	MB										◄	1
												29

Key: ◄ = Meeting

Fig. 3.1 Sample project plan

PROJECT BUDGET

CLIENT *Production Division*

PROJECT TITLE *Prep. of Job Descriptions*   PROJECT NUMBER *0041*   DAYS

WORK AREA	CONSULTANT						TOTAL
	MB	LC	JS				
Initial meeting	0·5						0·5
Draw up J D form	0·5						0·5
Job holder interviews		6	6				12
Department Head interviews	1	1	1				3
Progress meeting	1						1
Job description preparation	1	2	2				5
Further Dept Head IVs.	1	1	1				3
Progress meeting	1						1
Revision of job descriptions	0·5	0·5	1				2
Final meeting	1						1
Contingency time	1						1
TOTAL WORKTIME	8·5	10·5	11				30
AT DAILY RATE (£)	750	400	400				
	6375	4200	4400				£14,975

Fig. 3.2 Sample project budget

PROJECT EXPENSE BUDGET

EXPENSE AREA	DESCRIPTION	COST ESTIMATED
Travel	Rail Fares to Loamshire; 20@ £15	£300
Hotel	Hotel accomodation in Loamshire 10 nights at £50 per night	£500
Meals	(Included in hotel accom)	–
Report preparation	Preparation of descriptions, reports etc	£200
Other		
	TOTAL	£1,000

Fig. 3.3 Sample project expense budget

carry out the bulk of the interviewing and write up the job descriptions). The total time spent by each and the cost of this expressed as a standard fee rate are also shown.

Project expense budget

Fig. 3.3 simply shows all the estimated additional costs required to complete the project. As can be seen, these relate mostly to travel and accommodation costs which result from the requirement for job analysts to visit the company's second production site in Loamshire.

In this example, the project manager has completed the plan in 'freehand' manner, adhering only loosely to the layout of the forms themselves. This is not important; what really matters is that detailed thought has been given to the project, what it is likely to involve in terms of resources and how it should be managed. All this is essential preliminary work to the preparation of a formal proposal.

The proposal

The imaginary proposal letter set out in Fig. 3.4 relates to the Stonyshire Manufacturing Company project, the workplan for which is described in the previous section.

The key features of this proposal are:

- it is in the form of a letter: in the internal consulting context, this is usually likely to be a more appropriate format for a proposal than the frequently lengthy and elaborate reports prepared by professional consulting firms.
- it contains all the essential elements that need to be included, which we specified in Chapter One. These are: a summary of the background, a description of the client's requirements, a description of the approach to be taken, a statement of the actual and elapsed time requirements, details of the project team staffing and their roles, the fees and expenses that will be charged, the project deliverables and, crucially, the benefits to the client.
- the proposal is written in plain English and follows a logical structure. Technical terms and jargon are avoided. It is very specific as

Joe Albion
Production Director
Stonyshire Manufacturing Company
Loamshire Production Site

June 1994

Dear Joe

PREPARATION OF JOB DESCRIPTIONS

Following our meeting last week to discuss your requirements, I wish to set out how the company's Consulting Unit can help you in the important task of preparing a comprehensive set of job descriptions for the staff of your division. I am confident that the experienced team I have put together for this project will be able to complete the work to high standards and within the required timescale.

This proposal is structured as follows:
● background and requirements,
● our approach to the work,
● the experience of the project team,
● timescales and costs,
● conclusion.

BACKGROUND AND REQUIREMENTS
The company's Production Division currently operates from two sites, the main plant in Loamshire employing approximately 400 staff, and a further site in Stonyshire employing approximately 250 staff. Based on the information you have supplied me and my own scrutiny of the personnel records, there are 35 different job titles encompassing staff from production operative to plant supervisor, grouped within 10 different grades.

At present, no formal job descriptions exist for staff in the Production Division. This has caused a number of problems: in particular you believe that the job content of many posts has changed due to the introduction of new technology, meaning that they are incorrectly placed within their current grade. The preparation of sound job descriptions is also a main requirement for achievement of ISO9000 certification, which is currently being sought by the company.

Fig. 3.4 Sample consultancy proposal letter

You therefore require the preparation of comprehensive job descriptions for all posts and to a standard format. This will require:

- the development of a standard job description format suitable for the range of jobs in the Production Division,
- the interviewing of a number of job holders and managers to obtain details of jobs, carried out by trained job analysts,
- the preparation of job descriptions for all different jobs, using the standard format.

You also require a brief report on the methodology used, findings and any recommendations concerning job titles, reduction and consolidation of job categories where appropriate.

OUR APPROACH TO THE WORK
We would adopt a three-phase approach to this project, as follows:

- Phase 1: development of job description format, job holder interviews
- Phase 2: preparation and verification of job descriptions
- Phase 3: finalisation of descriptions, report on findings

Each of these phases is described below.

Phase 1: Job Description Format and Interviews
At an initial meeting with you and your two plant managers we would confirm the scope and work programme of the project, and confirm key facts relevant to our work. Following this meeting we would draw up a draft standard job description form, which we would discuss and agree with you. The form would be tailored to your specific requirements, and would conform to good practice in the preparation of job descriptions. In our experience, job descriptions should be no more than two pages in length and should specify the key features of the job, including:

- title of job holder,
- title of job holder's immediate manager,
- job purpose,
- main responsibilities,
- main authorities (for staff, materials, etc.),
- key contacts (e.g. with other staff, suppliers),
- decision-making requirements, and
- skills, experience and qualifications required.

In this phase we would also carry out the task of gathering information

Fig. 3.4 Continued

about all jobs within the division. Our approach would be to hold interviews with approximately 35 job holders (for each different job you have identified) using a structured questionnaire format. During these interviews we would cover all key features of the jobs in sufficient depth to complete the new job description forms.

We would also hold interviews with the five departmental heads in the division. The purpose of these interviews would be to confirm the details supplied by job holders and gain understanding of the reporting structures and organisation of work in the division.

We anticipate that these interviews would be between one and a half and two hours in length. At the end of this phase we would produce a brief interim report on progress and findings and hold a further meeting with you and your two plant managers to discuss this.

Phase 2: Preparation of Job Descriptions
Having obtained details of all different jobs within the division, we would then prepare job descriptions using the standard format. These would be grouped in departmental order. We would verify the content by submitting each group to the appropriate departmental head. We would hold further meetings with the departmental heads to confirm the details and explain any issues concerning specific jobs.

Phase 3: Finalisation of Descriptions, and Reporting
At the beginning of this phase we would hold a further meeting with you and your two plant managers to discuss any problems and issues encountered, including our recommendations concerning changes (e.g. to job titles, or the combination of two or more jobs into one description). Following preparation of the final descriptions, we would submit these to you with a brief report covering the methodology used, our findings and recommendations concerning issues such as future job titles and grading. We would wish to discuss this report with you at a final meeting.

Our Approach: Key Issues
We strongly recommend that a counterpart from the production division (possibly a unit manager or supervisor) is allocated to this project, to work alongside the job analysts and take part both in the fact-finding and preparation of job descriptions. This will help to ensure that understanding of our approach is maintained within the division, and will facilitate the

Fig. 3.4 Continued

process of amending descriptions in the future as jobs change.

We would wish to liaise closely with the Personnel Department in carrying out this project. As you know, a review of the Head Office grading structure is currently being undertaken by this department, and it will be important to ensure that our work is compatible with this review. I hope that this liaison may also help to build better relations between the Production Division and Personnel Department, which are currently acknowledged to be unsatisfactory.

THE EXPERIENCE OF THE PROJECT TEAM

As head of the company's Consulting Unit, I would be project manager of this exercise. I will therefore be responsible for ensuring that the work proceeds according to the agreed schedule, and to high quality standards. I will also hold main responsibility for liaison with you throughout the project.

As you know from our previous meetings, I have five years' experience as a consultant with a major professional practice before joining the company earlier this year. My main areas of specialism were the development of organisation structures and company strategies. I was responsible for the management of a number of major projects in the manufacturing sector, including the review of job content and working practices.

Two job analysts will be seconded to this project from the company's personnel department: **Julius Stewart** and **Louise Clarke**. They will be responsible for carrying out most of the job holder and manager interviews and preparation of job descriptions. They both have considerable experience of job analysis, and have both worked for periods of time within the Production Division as Management Trainees.

TIMESCALES AND COSTS

We could commence this work immediately on being given your authority to do so. We envisage the project requiring an elapsed timescale of 8–10 weeks, subject to the availability of your staff for meetings and interviews.

The fees we would charge for this work are based on the number of days worked by myself and the two job analysts, which in total we estimate to be 30 days. Based on this and the work programme set out above we estimate a total cost, excluding expenses, of £15,000. This assumes an input of ten days by a counterpart from the Production Division, which

Fig. 3.4 Continued

would cut down the required consultant time to some extent.

Expenses would be made up by the cost of travelling from Head Office to the Loamshire plant, hotel accommodation and document preparation costs. We estimate these costs would be £1,000, made up as follows:

- travel fares: £300
- overnight accommodation: £500
- document preparation: £200

Our fees would be submitted on a monthly basis and would be payable through the company's standard internal cost transfer system.

DELIVERABLES AND BENEFITS
In summary, the deliverables of this project would be:

- a standard job description form,
- full job descriptions, using the standard form, for all posts within the Production Division, and
- a report setting out the methodology used, issues arising and recommendations for modification to your job and grading structure.

A number of clear benefits would result from this project. In particular, you will be able to apply a fair grading and reward structure throughout the division, and will be able to carry out rationalisation of your current jobs to bring them more in line with your business needs. You will also be in a position to pursue your application for ISO9000.

I would like to thank you for inviting me to propose for this project. I am confident that the approach outlined, together with the experience of the job analysts in preparing job descriptions, will enable us to meet your requirements in full.

Should you require any further information, please do not hesitate to call me on extension 8836.

Regards

Mike Beranger
Consulting Unit

Fig. 3.4 Continued

to the actual work to be carried out in each phase, and the reporting arrangements. It is easy to read and should be readily understood.

- client involvement is emphasised, through the regular meetings with the Production Manager, involvement of managerial staff in verifying the job descriptions and, most importantly, use of a counterpart from the Production Division in the actual project work.
- the proposal is derived directly from the initial workplan, and reflects the approach taken and assumptions made in putting this together. It should be noted that the fees proposed are different from those calculated in the workplan set out earlier, however. This is because the consultant has decided on a fee rate that takes account of the client's ability/willingness to pay rather than charging the full 'scale rate'.

Because it contains all these features, the proposal establishes full understanding from the outset between the consultant and client, and stands as a crucial document which can be used for reference if the project goes ahead. It cannot be emphasised strongly enough that, for these reasons alone, no project should go ahead without a formal proposal having been presented to the client beforehand.

INTERVIEWING SKILLS IN THE CONSULTING CONTEXT

The ability to conduct effective interviews is a key skill required of all consultants, irrespective of the context in which they are working. Interviews with client staff and other people will be necessary throughout a project, particularly in the early stages when the relationship is still being built and information needs to be gathered before recommendations can be made.

Consider the imaginary workplan and proposal for the Stonyshire Manufacturing Company set out above. Assuming the project is accepted and goes ahead, it starts with an initial meeting with the Production Director and his two Plant Managers, 'to confirm the scope and work programme of the project and confirm key facts relevant to our work'. The first phase of the project also involves a series of interviews with approximately 35 job holders and the five departmental heads within the division. At a later stage in the work there is a further meeting with the Production Director and his two managers, and at the very end of the project a final meeting to discuss the recommendations in the consultant's report.

Each of these sets of interviews have different purposes, and requires a different approach:

- the initial meeting with the client is essentially a 'kick-off' interview with the main purpose of confirming the approach set out in the proposal, co-ordination between the client and the project team and discussing further the nature of the deliverables. It will also establish rapport with the client (in this instance, particularly with the two Plant Managers who are key client staff and with whom there may have been little contact before the proposal has been accepted).
- the job holder interviews, to be carried out by the two job analysts, are fact-finding sessions which have the purpose of obtaining as many details as possible about the jobs within the Production Division, in such a manner as to be readily written up onto job description forms.
- the departmental heads' interviews have the purpose of confirming and agreeing the content of the job descriptions, including reporting structures and organisation of work. They are potentially contentious, for example if there is substantial disagreement between the information given by job holders and the views of the departmental heads.
- the main purpose of the interview with the Production Director and Plant Managers at the beginning of Phase Three is to generate views and ideas concerning the way forward, particularly concerning any improvements to the organisation of work or the content of specific jobs that could benefit the Production Division.
- the purpose of the final interview is to 'sign off' the project, ensuring that the client understands and accepts the recommendations and is able to put them into practice.

The main features of each of these types of interview are set out below.

The 'kick-off' interview

Particularly where the interview is with people with whom the consultant has had little or no previous contact, it is essential to state at the outset the purpose of meeting them, why this is important and what you expect to gain from it. As a main objective is to build confidence and rapport, it is important for there to be no misunderstandings at the outset. Remember that you are seeking the support of these people, the interview is at least as important to you as it is to them.

In terms of content, the interview should focus on practical matters and considerations. At this stage, you probably have only a general knowledge of the problems and issues you will encounter in carrying out your work, and you will need a better handle on these before you begin the work. Therefore, topics to be covered should include:

- fact-finding: for example who are the best people in the organisation you need to see, where are they based, when are they likely to be available? Are there any other sources of information that would be valuable to you? Are there any special factors (e.g. political or personal issues, or areas of confidentiality) that you need to know?
- expectations: not only what the client expects in terms of deliverables, but what hopes and expectations may be raised throughout the organisation as the project proceeds. It is important to know this if these expectations are to be managed properly.
- administration: including any clerical or secretarial support being provided by the client, involvement of counterparts and office facilities. You should also agree the next steps to the project in detail, so that everyone knows what will happen and the consultants can prepare their next course of action.

The kick-off interview will have been successful if you have established friendly and businesslike relations with your main client counterpart(s), are aware of their expectations and are in a position to proceed without delay with the project work.

The fact-finding interview

Interviews of this type form the core of many engagements carried out by external consultants, even where the project is essentially 'process consulting' in nature. It could be argued that for an internal consultant the need for an extensive fact-finding interview pro-gramme will be less, as the consultant should, if he/she is doing the job properly, already have acquired a thorough knowledge of the organisation. However there will be many situations where an internal consultant still needs to carry out fact-finding interviews to gain detailed information – the Stonyshire Production Company project being a good example.

The objective of any fact-finding interview is, obviously, to gain as much detailed information as possible about the topic under con-sideration: the nature of someone's job, the steps in a process, the checks and balances in a system. In addition to verbal information, it can be vital in many situations to obtain copies of forms or manuals used, examples of work produced and records kept (e.g. productivity figures, quality standards or fault response times). Particularly where large numbers of people are being interviewed, it is essential to prepare a general outline of the topics to be covered to refer to during the interview.

Because the person being interviewed may only have a vague idea in advance of what the interview is about (and may, in many circum-stances be unused to expressing themselves in an interview situation or feel threatened by it) two things are particularly important:

- putting the person at ease, and clarifying at the outset the informa-tion required; and
- conducting the interview in a clear and logical way, so that ques-tions are readily understood. In this context, 'open' rather than 'closed' questions should be used. It may be necessary from time to time to confirm your understanding, and to check information either by repeating a question in a different way or referring back directly to information given earlier. Even in well conducted inter-views, circumstances may still arise where the person being inter-viewed simply does not understand the relevance of information being sought; patience and perseverance are necessary!

Notes should always be taken during a fact-finding interview, to ensure that all facts and the context in which they have been given are retained. It is rare for people being interviewed to object to note-taking, as long as they are informed before you begin.

Finally, where a number of consultants are involved in fact-finding, it is important for them to co-ordinate their activities to make sure that the same people are not being asked the same or similar questions. Nothing 'turns off' interviewees more than the feeling they are not being listened to, are not trusted or that the information they are giving is of no value.

The confirming/agreeing interview

Interviews of this type are sometimes necessary to confirm information received from other sources before proceeding with a project. Usually, the purpose is not so much to 'check up' on the truth of what others are telling you as to ensure that there is a working basis for development of options, deliverables and other recommendations. In the Stonyshire Manufacturing Company case, for example, it is absolutely essential to have the agreement of departmental managers to the details of work carried out by their staff before enshrining this in job descriptions.

These interviews usually involve a considerable amount of information being fed back by the consultant to be checked by the interviewee. It is important that this information is expressed clearly, making use of diagrams or statistics where appropriate. It is important also to check periodically that the interviewee agrees with the information being given.

Particular problems can arise where the interviewee simply does not agree with information given by someone else interviewed previously. Where this happens, it may be necessary to go back over old ground to check facts. Ultimately, if disagreement between different client staff persists, the only course of action is to bring this to the attention of the main client contact for resolution.

The 'brainstorm' interview

Interviews of this type are likely to be infrequent during the course of a project, but play a vital part in its success. They take place at key stages in the work programme and usually involve the main client contacts. They involve a two-way flow of ideas between the consultant and the client, to cement relations between them and take recommendations forward. They can be very valuable in getting the client to think for themselves, involve them in decisions and build their commitment.

From the consultant's point of view, the main purposes of the brainstorm interview are:

- to put forward options, views and ideas developed from previous research and investigation, and test them out; and
- to test out the views of the client, exploring their own ideas and preferences and their willingness to accept change.

Frequently, the consultant will be using the interview to present his/her own ideas to the client for the first time, therefore thorough preparation is essential. The consultant must be able, during the interview, to express views and options clearly and justify opinions and preferences. All relevant facts and figures should be readily to hand for reference. Some time should be spent in advance of the interview in anticipating the client's likely response to contentious issues, and to working out how to deal with this.

In most circumstances, it is advisable to issue the client with a brief report or paper before the meeting takes place, setting out the consultant's main findings and, if appropriate, preferred options. This enables the client to think issues through in advance, and come to the meeting with ideas and opinions better formed.

During the interview, the consultant should 'run the show'; this means leading the discussion, making use of visual aids or other support material as appropriate. Use of flipcharts is recommended, to record ideas, agreements and action points that form during the course of the discussion. Some key 'do's and don'ts' are:

- be prepared to explain your points of view carefully and in detail. This is particularly important where you are recommending a preferred solution, where you may need to justify your position to listeners who are sceptical or reluctant to accept change.

- don't be too dogmatic or unwilling to accept other points of view. Above all, don't be drawn into conflict with your client. External consultants can, on occasions, be far too inflexible in accepting that their clients can have alternative ideas that will work; don't fall into the trap of believing that you **always** know better than your client does. Listen carefully to what your client tells you, and be prepared to modify your approach if there is value in their opinions.
- try to reach a consensus on recommendations and action points. However, don't force this; the client may need more time to consider your proposals, or issues may arise during the discussion that need resolution before firm recommendations can be made.
- conversely, on occasions you may need to restrain your clients from running too far, too fast. Get them to think carefully about what is achievable, how they would implement recommendations, the possible constraints and benefits arising.

The brainstorm interview will be a success if it develops the ideas that you, the consultant, have formed and enables you to make progress with the agreement and involvement of the client.

The 'sign-off' interview

This type of interview takes place at the end of the project, or at the end of key stages in a very large project. It is always held between the consultant and the main client contact, and may also involve the project sponsor if this person is different from the client. The purpose is to confirm formal acceptance of the consultant's recommendations, ensure these are fully understood and agree necessary implementation plans.

Above all, at this stage in the project there should be no surprises – neither for the client nor the consultant. Progress made and recommendations given should have been thoroughly explored during previous meetings. You may however be aware of unresolved issues, or differences of opinion between yourself and the client. Equally, you may be doubtful about the client's commitment or ability to implement agreed action plans. It is amazing sometimes how clients get 'cold feet' when they are required to become accountable for implementing change.

As with the brainstorming interview, anticipation of potential problem areas is absolutely vital, and you will need to prepare in advance a strategy to overcome these. If a detailed action plan has not been supplied as part of the project, you may need to prepare one for the meeting itself. Where particularly sensitive issues are involved you will need to think through how to 'sell' your ideas to people who, for one reason or another, may be reluctant to accept them.

As with the brainstorming interview, you need to be 'in charge'. This means deciding on when to raise particular issues; emphasising the advantages of your proposals and resolving practical matters concerning implementation. When agreement is reached, you should confirm this straight away. The client may need pushing – be prepared to do this, without pushing so hard as to upset them. Knowledge of the people you are dealing with, and recognising the right time to push for a decision, are essential.

More than any other meeting or interview, the sign-off interview will need agreements and action plans to be carefully recorded, and issued to the client in written form as soon as possible after the interview has been concluded.

General interviewing skills

Learning and applying effective interviewing techniques is a skill that needs to be acquired by many managers and staff – not just consultants. Interviewing skills courses giving instruction in these techniques are readily available, many using 'guinea pigs' to act as interviewees so that delegates can practise in a realistic environment, and closed circuit television so that performances in practice interviews can be played back and learning points reinforced.

Although the subject of interviewing skills is too general to be covered here in detail, it is worth briefly considering some of the main skills areas, in particular interview preparation, different forms of questioning to use during the interview itself, and what to do afterwards.

Interview preparation

Preparation is required before any interview takes place, to ensure all areas of investigation are covered properly, and to anticipate problems and issues. At the very least, thought needs to be given to the objectives being sought and practical considerations such as how long the interview will take and where it should be held. Where a number of similar interviews with different people are being held (common with fact-finding interviewing) it is usually necessary to draw up a checklist of topics to be covered. There may also be topics to be avoided. Any potential issues or problems should be anticipated and suitable responses devised. There may be a need to issue documents to the person being interviewed, or prepare handouts or other information to be issued during the interview itself.

Interview question skills

Using appropriate forms of questioning is a core interviewing skill. The most common forms are:

- **open questions:** (How . .? Why . .? Give me an example of . .? Describe to me . .?) This is the most widely recommended form of questioning, enabling the interviewer to explore and gather information. It provides the opportunity for the person being interviewed to respond expansively rather than give a simple yes' or 'no' answer.
- **closed questions:** (Do you have staff directly reporting to you? Have you been to the Stonyshire plant?) These questions invite a simple yes/no response; they are of little use in exploring information but can be effective in checking facts or understanding.
- **leading questions:** (It's a good idea to delegate responsibility, isn't it?) The interviewee is invited to agree with a statement made by the interviewer – dangerous unless you are specifically testing the interviewee's reaction.
- **controlling questions:** (You've told me about your leisure interests. Now can we go back to your experience as a shift leader within the group?) These questions can be vital to bring an interview back on track.

- **probing questions:** (Could you tell me more about that?) Useful for building on information already given, but where more is required for complete understanding.
- **reflecting back questions:** (So you think responsibility for equipment is an important aspect of production jobs?) Useful for backtracking to a topic where insufficient information was originally obtained, these are usually 'closed' questions but can be followed up immediately to open up the topic (You do? Can you tell me more about that?).
- **multiple questions:** (Did you say earlier you're responsible for the lifting gear? You must consider that a big responsibility: could you tell me more about it?) Any combination of two or more questions, these are likely to confuse the interviewee and should be avoided at all costs.

In most situations it is advisable to ask the interviewee, before concluding the interview, if they would object to a follow-up visit or call in case anything further needs to be discussed – few people object to this.

After the interview

It is essential to check that all the required information has been obtained as soon as possible. Notes taken during the interview should be reviewed and checked to ensure there are no important omissions. It may be necessary to write up interview notes for ease of reference, particularly if they are to be read by a third party. Any areas that are unclear should be noted and, if possible, should be referred back to the interviewee for clarification.

Action points should be recorded separately and those responsible for carrying them out should be informed. It may be necessary in some circumstances to brief others verbally about the outcome of the interview; this should be done as soon as possible after the interview has taken place.

DEVELOPING AND MOUNTING EFFECTIVE SURVEYS

Surveys are an extremely valuable way of obtaining consistent and wide-ranging information, and can therefore form an important part of a consulting project. They can be used both internally (e.g. a staff attitude survey) or externally (e.g. to obtain comparative data from other organisations, or data concerning customer satisfaction levels). Knowing how to conduct an effective survey is, therefore, a key skill for an internal consultant to learn.

Surveys may take many forms and it is important to decide on the most appropriate method of collecting information before going ahead. Some of the most common forms of survey in the internal consulting context are:

- **paper questionnaire:** circulated or issued by post, this is probably the most commonly used form where information is sought from many different sources. Questionnaire design is most important, particularly where respondents have no direct interest in the results. Broadly speaking, the questionnaire form should not take too long to complete, and most questions should require only a simple response (e.g. ticking of a yes/no' box or selection of an answer from a multiple choice). Used effectively, these questionnaires can provide highly consistent and unbiased data that reflects the respondent's genuine, unbiased views. The disadvantages are that response rates may be low, and respondents may misunderstand the purpose of questioning or the questions themselves.

- **telephone surveys:** any consultant using this method must be prepared to spend many hours making calls, many of which will be fruitless. Nevertheless, telephone surveys can be highly effective, both to obtain 'hard' data and 'softer' information such as understanding and opinions. It is important to develop a standard questionnaire format for the telephone interview, to ensure both consistency and effective data analysis. A major benefit is the depth of information that can sometimes be obtained – it is amazing how much detail people will willingly divulge during a direct telephone conversation with a complete stranger.

- **information exchange 'clubs':** in some circumstances it can be beneficial for organisations to group together to exchange data. Contact can be on an informal basis (counterparts in the different organisations simply phoning each other to find out information) or more formally through the medium of a periodic survey. This form of co-operation is most common amongst organisations in the same industry grouping, for example to exchange information on salaries and employment conditions for staff. They are an excellent means of building networks and thereby finding out both 'hard' and 'soft' data concerning competitors and other institutions.

- **'buttonholing':** approaching customers with a clipboard as they enter or leave client premises is a technique used in market research that can sometimes be appropriate, particularly when seeking qualitative information concerning issues such as service standards. It is best to stick to a limited number of fairly straight-forward, open questions: 'What do you think of the layout of this branch?' 'How satisfied are you with the advice you are given by customer advisers?' On the whole the technique is probably best left in the hands of professional consumer researchers.

- **secret visits:** visits or telephone calls by researchers posing as customers is another technique sometimes used in consumer research. Again, it can provide valuable qualitative data but should not be undertaken without professional training. It can create a lot of resentment amongst staff if they find out what's going on.

In order to gain the greatest benefit from surveys, it is often worth carrying out follow-up interviews with a small selection of respondents; either a random sample or those who have expressed particularly interesting views in completed questionnaires or telephone surveys. An alternative is to hold focus groups in which a number of survey respondents are brought together for a meeting at which they are able to expand on and exchange their views freely. This can often add greater detail or important qualitative information to the raw data, or put in context the trends coming through from survey information.

On completing a survey it is sound practice to compile a summary of the information obtained and issue this to all respondents. They will frequently find the survey results of interest, and may be more amenable to further approaches for information should the need arise.

Two further points to consider in mounting surveys:

- where there is a lot of information to be analysed it can be beneficial, as well as cost effective, to use a data analysis company. These organisations are capable of analysing a mass of complex data very quickly and flexibly, and of presenting it in different forms as requested by the client. Their fees are usually reasonable (in some cases, less than the cost of analysing the information 'in house').
- surveys should not be used as a smokescreen for 'industrial espionage'. If you are seeking sensitive information from competitors or other sources, you should be completely open about who you are, why you want the information and what you intend to do with it. Obtaining data by underhand means may bring short-term advantages, but is highly risky and may in the long term jeopardise your own reputation or that of your organisation. Moreover, it is simply dishonest (and accordingly against the codes of practice applied by all reputable firms of management consultants).

In order to illustrate the principles and practices of conducting surveys – particularly the different types of questionnaire and their uses – we set out below examples of projects involving, respectively, a circulated paper questionnaire and a telephone questionnaire. These are probably the two most common forms an internal consultant is likely to use. The examples show how simple, well structured surveys can produce a good response and much valuable information for the consultant.

Example 1:

An Internal Staff Attitude Survey

Imagine the following scenario: the senior management of a national food retail company was concerned about the attitudes of staff towards working for the company. In order to gain more information about the areas of greatest concern and the depth of ill-feeling amongst staff, the company's internal consulting unit was commissioned to carry out an attitude survey and report to the Board on findings.

Approach to the survey

The internal consulting unit was ideally placed to carry out this work, as it was regarded throughout the company as independent from senior management and therefore impartial. During initial discussions with the client, the following approach was agreed:

- development of a short questionnaire, to be issued by internal mail to all 3,000 staff on a confidential basis, covering the areas of most concern: working for the company, pay and benefits, teamworking and job security.
- analysis of the information from returned questionnaires by an external data analysis company.
- a brief written report on the survey findings to be presented to the Board; and a summary of the findings to be issued to staff in a newsletter.

The questionnaire developed by the consulting unit, agreed by the Board and issued to staff is set out in Figs. 3.5 and 3.6. Some key features of this are:

- the covering letter, from the Chief Executive, emphasises the purpose of the survey and that information given is totally confidential.
- clear instructions are given on how to respond to the questions in the survey.
- completed questionnaires are returned direct to a data analysis company, in envelopes provided.
- the questions themselves are clear and require only a simple response from a multiple choice list. There are only 16 questions in total, so reading the instructions and completing the questionnaire should take a few minutes only.

STAFF ATTITUDE SURVEY

From: The Chief Executive

To: All Staff

Date: April 1994

Subject: **Staff Attitudes and Concerns**

As you are all aware, the last year has been a difficult one for the company. Increased competition, the unprofitability of some of our smaller stores and the continuing store refurbishment programme have brought about many changes that have affected us all. I know from my informal visits to stores throughout the country that you have many concerns regarding your future in the company. In order to understand these better, we have decided to conduct an attitude survey to assess staff views.

Please therefore complete the attached questionnaire and return it, as soon as possible, to our data analysis company in the envelope provided. The questionnaire covers four specific areas: working for the company, pay and benefits, teamworking and job security. Your response will be totally anonymous, you are not asked to sign the questionnaire or give your name when you return it.

The results of the questionnaire will be collated and a summary will be issued to all staff later this year. We intend to issue similar surveys in future years, to establish how your views change over time.

This survey is a major element of our programme to improve communications with staff, and respond better to your concerns. Please, therefore, take the time to complete and return the questionnaire.

Thanking you in advance for doing this,

The Chief Executive.

Fig. 3.5 Chief Executive's covering letter for Staff Attitude Survey

STAFF ATTITUDE SURVEY

This questionnaire is totally anonymous
and no individual responses to it will be identified

Completing Instructions   Circle the number that best reflects your
response to the question. The numbers
correspond to the following responses:

1   Agree
2   Neither agree nor disagree
3   Disagree

For example: I like to wear smart clothes   1   2   3

By circling number 1 the respondent indicates he/she agrees with the
statement.

Section 1: Working for the company

1. I enjoy my work in the store/warehouse   1   2   3

2. I find my work sufficiently demanding   1   2   3

3. My job leaves me enough time
   for my family life and other interests   1   2   3

4. I receive recognition for doing my job well   1   2   3

5. Overall, I am satisfied with working for the company   1   2   3

Section 2: Team Working

6. People in my store/warehouse work well as a team   1   2   3

7. My colleagues in the store/warehouse
   help me do my job well   1   2   3

8. There is good liaison between my store/warehouse
   and other operational units   1   2   3

Fig. 3.6 Staff Attitude Survey questionnaire

9. I am usually informed by head office
    of changes in the company that affect me   1   2   3

Section 3: Pay and Benefits

10. I receive a fair wage for the work I do   1   2   3

11. I am satisfied with my fringe benefits
    (e.g. discount scheme, social club, holiday pay)   1   2   3

12. I have opportunities to increase my basic earnings
    (e.g. overtime, weekend working)   1   2   3

13. I have opportunities for promotion in the company 1   2   3

Section 4: Job Security

14. I believe my job is secure   1   2   3

15. I am worried about future changes
    that may affect my job   1   2   3

16. The company's redeployment policy is an effective
    means of minimising staff reductions   1   2   3

Background Information

This information will allow more detailed analysis of the questionnaire responses, and will therefore make the results more useful. Please therefore complete the section below.

Completing this section will not prejudice your anonymity in returning the questionnaire.

I work in a ...
    high street store
    discount store
    superstore
    warehouse

Fig. 3.6 Continued

I am ...

        male

        female

My age is ...

        below 25

        25 to 40

        over 40

My grade is ...

        1 to 5

        6 to 9

        10 to 12

        Store/warehouse management

Please add overleaf any other comments you have concerning subjects covered in this questionnaire.

Thank you for completing this questionnaire.

Fig. 3.6 Continued

- respondents are invited to add any comments they may have on the subjects covered by the questionnaire. This may reveal important concerns not specifically included, or add 'qualitative' information to the data.

How the survey progressed

Following issue to all staff, completed questionnaires were returned to the data analysis company. By the 'cut-off' date (sensibly, the company had set this at one week after the return date indicated to staff in the questionnaire) 60% of staff had responded. This is about what was expected, and a sufficiently large sample for the results to be regarded as having high statistical accuracy. The data analysis company broke down the responses by question and by operating

HOTEL TELEPHONE SURVEY – Staff Manager/Head of Training

Introduction

Good morning/afternoon

My name is ... from Loamshire College of Further Education. I am carrying out some research for the college into the attitudes towards training amongst hotels and caterers. This is because we are considering launching a new course in hotel and catering. I am contacting a number of hotels, chosen on a random basis, to ask about their views on staff training and their future commitment to training in general.

I anticipate the interview will take about 15 to 20 minutes. All information you give me will be entirely confidential. Are you willing to be interviewed?

1. Background Information
a) Your name
b) Your position
c) Hotel
d) Date
e) Describe the range of your services (e.g. hotel only: hotel and restaurant: main clientele)
f) Annual turnover
g) Number of staff employed

2. Commitment to Training
a) Size of training budget in current year
b) Is this budget bigger than last year?
c) Is the budget likely to increase or decrease in the future?
d) Main focus of training:
catering
hotel reception
hotel management
customer care
other
e) What are the main growth areas for training?
f) What training resources do you have (e.g. own training centre: dedicated training staff
g) How is training carried out?

Fig. 3.7 Hotel Telephone Survey questionnaire

off-job courses

coaching

self-study

day release

evening/weekend study

h)   Training providers:
own training centre
external colleges
professional bodies
external private training institutions
other

i)   Is it important that training leads to a qualification?

j)   Which of your current training programmes lead to qualifications,
and what are these qualifications?

3.   Use of Colleges as Training Providers

If you use colleges:

a)   What courses are currently provided by colleges?

b)   What are the training methods?

c)   What is the duration of courses?

d)   What categories and how many of your staff are involved?

e)   What are the strengths of these courses?

f)   What are their weaknesses?

g)   What problems have you encountered with colleges?

h)   Do the colleges you use tailor their courses to your needs?

i)   How is the course progress made by staff assessed?

j)   How is the success of courses themselves assessed?

k)   Will use of colleges for training increase/decrease/stay the same in
future? (explore why, anticipated new areas etc.)

If you *don't* use colleges:

a)   Why not?

b)   Any contact with colleges as training providers in the past?

c)   Any 'bad experiences'?

d)   Would you consider using colleges in the future? (explore why, etc.)

4.   Incentives to Staff to Undertake Training

Which of the following incentives for staff to undertake training exist?

Fig. 3.7 Continued

study sponsorship
exam success awards
promotion
pay increases
other

5. **Staff Attitudes to Training**

a) What is the attitude of your staff to training?
b) What is the attitude of your staff to obtaining qualifications?

Thank you for the time you have spent in answering these questions.

Fig. 3.7 Continued

between the staff of different divisions.

On receipt of the analysed data, the internal consultancy pre-pared a report for the Board, including an executive summary. This gave details of the statistical methods and accuracy, response rates and results in each of the key question areas (working for the company, pay and benefits, etc.) A one-page newsletter was pre-pared for the staff, summarising the results.

The survey information was regarded by the Board as sufficiently important to commission further work in the areas of team building and communication. The decision was made to repeat the survey every two years, to monitor changes in staff attitudes over time.

Example 2
Investigating the Market for a New Service

Here, a college of further education was considering launching a new course in the field of hotel catering. Before developing the course, however, the college wished to determine if there was a real market for such a qualification. An internal consultant was called in to advise on how to obtain this information.

Approach to the survey

The internal consultant recommended telephone interviews with a range of hotel chains, aimed at finding out as much information as possible about training practices and attitudes to externally provided training. It was agreed that a standard questionnaire would be developed, to be followed in conducting all interviews. The consultant estimated it would be necessary to approach approximately 150 catering managers in order to obtain a representative sample of 50 hotels. The consultant also recommended that a sample of five respondents be visited in person to gain more details about training plans.

The telephone questionnaire prepared by the consultant for this exercise is set out overleaf. Some key features of it are:

- it begins with a standard introduction setting out the purposes behind the research and how long the telephone interview is likely to take.
- it has five separate sections, which move from the general ('Background Information') to the specific ('Staff Attitudes to Training') in a logical order.
- it seeks both hard data (e.g. numbers of catering staff) and soft data (attitudes of catering staff to qualifications).

How the survey progressed

A major problem the consultant encountered in carrying out the survey was establishing contact with the best person in the hotels approached to give information. In some cases this proved impossible and as a result it was necessary to add to the original target population of 150 hotels.

However, the required number of 50 respondents was eventually achieved. Five catering managers who gave particularly interesting responses were subsequently visited to gain more details about their approach to training. All information obtained was incorporated into a report that set out clearly the main features hotels were seeking in commissioning training.

A summary of the results of the survey was subsequently sent to all catering managers who took part. Apart from anything else, this proved to be a good marketing exercise – the college having decided, on the basis of the research, to go ahead with development of a new training course.

From time to time it may be that, as a consultant, you are asked to take part in a questionnaire or survey conducted by another organisation. If so, there are a number of points to be considered before agreeing:

- ensure that the information being sought is something your organisation is happy to divulge: this may mean checking with senior management before going ahead. Ensure, also, that there is a valid reason for the research, and that there is not some ulterior motive such as competitor information or marketing.
- identify the benefits to your organisation. These may be direct (e.g. access to a database of useful information) or indirect (e.g. prestige associated with taking part in a reputable survey).
- ask for details of the results. If the survey is bona fide the organisers should be able to supply you with at least a summary of the data.
- ask if the data you will supply will remain confidential or will be available either to staff of the organisation carrying out the research or other participants. Equally, you may wish to know whether the specific information supplied by other participants will be identifiable or not.
- if you are considering taking part in an information exchange 'club', you should find out how many other organisations are participating, who they are and whether the data they provide is of any interest to you. There is little point in taking part in a survey where there are insufficient participants to provide statistically valid conclusions, or where the methods of information-gathering are inadequate. Ideally, participant information should be screened by the survey organisers to identify any inconsistencies or misunderstanding.

CHECKING AND ANALYSING INFORMATION

This is a faithful description of a conversation between consultant and client, which occurred during a meeting at which an interim report was presented:

Client: 'Your report is interesting, but there's one thing here on page one . . . you say that we recruit most of our scientists from Cumbria and Devon . . . whatever made you put that?'

Consultant: 'Well . . . I'm sure that you said that in one of our earlier interviews . . .'

Client: 'Said that? That's nonsense! Cumbria yes, but we've never recruited anyone from Devon . . .'

A trivial example of a piece of unchecked information, perhaps, but one that in this instance was damaging to the credibility of the consultant at a critical point in the project. More seriously, information that has not been verified or analysed properly can set a consultant in completely the wrong direction in the development of recommendations. Remember, the term 'information' encompasses more than just established facts; it includes estimates and guesstimates, views and opinions, forecasts and projections which come from many different sources and may be conflicting or misleading. There is a prime responsibility on the consultant to corroborate all information received rather than simply accepting it at face value.

Information checking has already been described to some extent in the context of interviewing skills. In particular:

- the 'confirming/agreeing interview', as described, involves feeding back information received from an earlier source to ascertain if it is generally agreed or is open to question.
- during an interview, it can be valuable to confirm information either by asking the same question in a different way or referring back to a topic discussed earlier ('Can you remind me of your view concerning . . .').

- during the course of a series of fact-finding interviews a similar set of questions will be asked of many different people. This gives the opportunity, in going through interview notes, to check which items of information are universally agreed and which are not.
- follow-up interviews can be arranged to revisit topics where the consultant is unclear of the facts, or where subsequent information has been received from a different source which conflicts with that given earlier.

In some cases, it is advisable to verify information given during interviews with 'official', written data. This is particularly so where the interviewee may have a personal reason for distorting the facts or giving only half the story. For example, a manager who feels under threat may be tempted to massage statistics concerning performance standards; the actual records should be checked. People describing their position in an organisation structure often give a false picture of their reporting relationships, to emphasise their own importance; their account should be compared with official organisation charts published by the company.

Where a number of staff have been involved in information gathering, it is vital that they meet regularly to exchange information and discuss any discrepancies. For example, going back to the Stonyshire Manufacturing Company project, two job analysts are involved in carrying out the fact-finding interviews. These analysts should maintain contact on a daily basis, and should, on completion of the interview programme, have a full meeting to discuss thoroughly the main features of each of the jobs under review. It is certain that this meeting will reveal conflicting information such as overlaps in responsibility and inconsistent authority levels between jobs. These conflicts must be recorded and verified before final job descriptions can be prepared.

It is perhaps never more important to check information received than when dealing with potential suppliers of goods or services, who are being considered as contractors. Frequently, the person giving information will be a salesperson who wishes to present as favourable a picture as possible. The best approach is to obtain independent verification through a user, either by obtaining references or, ideally, seeing things at first hand. If possible, the user should be selected by you rather than the salesperson. User visits can be a vital part of systems selection projects, where understanding of the capabilities and practicalities of software packages is so important.

Analysis of factual data can be greatly facilitated by use of a spreadsheet such as Lotus or Excel: spreadsheet modelling is a key skill for the internal consultant to learn. Non-factual information cannot be 'modelled' in this way and requires a less formal approach. However it can still be valuable to classify information in a standard format, to make comparisons between sets of data and draw conclusions from research. Tables are of help in this respect, as comparative information obtained from different sources can be more easily studied to pick out the key features, including similarities and differences in approach.

Finally, remember the benefit of using a data analysis company when there is a mass of complex survey information to be considered. Their sophisticated statistical techniques can present the data in many different forms, highlighting key considerations such as reliability and validity levels.

4

THE SIX KEY TASKS FOR SUCCESSFUL INTERNAL CONSULTING

In this chapter we examine the essential areas of project management. These include:

- delivering on time and to budget;
- managing staff engaged on the project;
- obtaining feedback from the client and testing client satisfaction;
- monitoring and measuring progress towards objectives;
- spotting opportunities to 'sell on';
- spotting danger signals.

Project management is not easy. It requires qualities that include tact, perseverance, self-belief and above all adherence to the fundamental principle that your objective is to meet the client's needs. Clients can waver in their resolve: you may need during a project to remind them of what you are trying to achieve and their responsibilities in helping you towards this. You will need to ask yourself similar questions: am I still on course to meet the deliverables of the project? How am I doing against the original workplan? Moreover, if you are managing other consultants during the project you will have to ask similar questions of their contributions as well.

DELIVERING ON TIME AND TO BUDGET

The previous chapter explored the significance of terms of reference and the need before embarking on a consulting project to scope out what is required, when and the means by which the consultancy assistance will be delivered. Whether one is managing oneself only or a large consulting team, this is a critical dimension of the practise of consultancy. In today's business environment it is increasingly the case that a consultancy project needs to be undertaken during a particular 'window of opportunity'. It follows that there can be a potential conflict between what needs to be done and how it needs to be done if you are to conclude the exercise with a 'satisfied' client. As in all aspects of consulting, effective expectation management is crucial:

- what does your client expect?
- by when?
- by what means?
- and how will the client and yourself know when you've got there?

What constitutes the 'window of consultancy opportunity' will vary dramatically. Effective groundwork before the project starts will hopefully highlight the context in which the exercise sits, but this is only the beginning.

Delivery on time

Whilst your proposal will have been based on a structured assessment of what you believe to be required, until a project starts it is in a very real sense merely theoretical. As all consultants know, the unexpected can happen at any time during any project. As General Eisenhower noted 'planning is essential but plans are useless'. So whilst the development of a cogent proposal and engagement plan are critical to success, managing a consulting project requires both vigilance and second-guessing if anticipated outcomes are to be achieved.

Why do problems occur? The most common reasons are:

- poor project management;
- scope creep;
- work being overlooked;
- insufficient client support/resources;
- workplan not realistic.

Poor project management

Your proposal has been accepted! Having won the project, a 'kick-off' meeting with the client is a key event. Many consultants have been undone by failing to create an impression of being in control of events during the first few days of a project. The following can help:

- think carefully about how to introduce yourself, to whom and when. Take account of the hierarchy within your client's organisation.
- look at staff lists, noticeboards, telephone directories, in-house magazines, and so on. This will give you a useful check against the information obtained during the pre-project research. It is surprising how many allegedly up-to-date organisation charts are in reality months out of date. You can't afford to slip up early on by addressing someone by the wrong job title. Equally, be sensitive to how requests for this sort of information may be received. Comments such as 'the last time consultants asked for that information was just before a redundancy' will not help your credibility.
- consider making an initial presentation about the project. Depending on the circumstances this could range from the Board to the entire workforce. For example, a business process review, requiring the commitment of the entire workforce might well necessitate large-scale presentations to allow everyone the opportunity to ask questions and see the consultants. Moreover, such an event is in itself a clear signal about wanting to get people involved. A project involving total quality might well require a meeting at Board level to ensure that the Board understand exactly what will be required of them during the project.
- 'Walk the talk'. Some consultants get 'desk bound' very easily in a project. There is no substitute for going out for a look at the environment upon which your work will impact and meeting the people who actually do the work. Many concerns will come out at an informal meeting by a vending machine which would never be signalled at a more formal meeting.
- learn what you can discreetly about interpersonal relationships. This may be less troublesome for an internal consultant in theory. In reality there may be acute suspicion about disclosure to an

'insider'.

- check on the working hours and holidays of those client staff you will need access to. Some clients will assure you at the proposal stage that you have access to whoever you want, when you want. They may forget overseas sales visits, projects, sabbaticals and other factors which may prevent access to key people as planned.
- At the outset confirm your regular reporting meetings as defined in your proposal and workplan and stick to them as far as possible.
- Ask the client **who else you** might need to see and why.
- Arrange for people to know where your office is and how they can contact you. Be aware that the office will signal to everyone your operating style, therefore a disorganised, chaotic work area will not heighten confidence in your professionalism.

Scope creep

Project management starts as soon as the client accepts your proposal. Continually refer back to the proposal and your workplan. Even very experienced consultants can get sidetracked by an unexpected request from a client.

Example: During a review of the effectiveness of a personnel department the client asked 'do you think you could give me some ideas on improving the way our performance appraisal process works – it should need no more than a few hours'.

Whilst the performance appraisal process was a key linkage in the interface between the personnel department and the rest of the organisation, revising the process was not built into the project proposal. Discussion with the client reconciled his natural desire for progress on all fronts with the need to accomplish what was the first priority on schedule. It was agreed that any review of performance appraisal would be postponed until the recommendations of the department review were complete. The consultants were subsequently engaged to conduct this work which, far from taking a few hours, took six more days.

Apart from monitoring adherence to terms of reference, you will need to ensure that things are done in the way you anticipated, and if not, that the consequences are clearly understood and communicated to the client.

Example: During an exercise to define managerial competencies it became clear that a key aspect had been overlooked by both the consultant and the client. Part of the answer could be provided by a senior executive now based in another division outside the UK. The individual concerned, the client, and the consultant all believed his input would be valuable but the cost had not been anticipated in the project budget. In the event there was no problem since there was detailed discussion of the implications of any extra work upon both the budget and the project schedule.

Work being overlooked

In a large project, involving a number of interdependent phases, effective planning can help to ensure that what you have committed to do actually happens. Without an adequate process to monitor progress how will you cope with the following:

- a stream of work being 'forgotten' because key client staff were not available at the right time to provide data; or
- the rationale of a cost-benefit analysis being questioned because the impact on a particular location had been neglected.

Without constant reference to your terms of reference such things can and do happen.

Insufficient client support/resources

Experienced consultants will check and recheck that promised support will actually materialise. It is important that very early in the project any shortfall in anticipated support is communicated very clearly to your client. You must record in writing the impact of this upon the project and the cost of any alternative. Frequently the cost of buying a service on the open market will convince your client that they really should provide some secretarial support. The absence of the required level of support is both more problematical and nebulous. It can take many forms, ranging from the non-appearance of the project sponsor at a kick-off meeting, to access to particular information being denied. An example would be the team of consultants hired to conduct a training needs analysis who were refused access to key business planning data. Again the consultant must immediately emphasise the consequences of this on the quality of their output. If you wait until your final report is presented to raise this as an issue, do not be surprised if your client expresses amazement: 'why didn't you let me know'.

Workplan not realistic

A workplan based on optimism rather than experience may indeed cause delivery problems. For a new consultant 'guesstimating' the time a particular project will take can be very tricky. In part, error can be avoided by breaking the project into discrete tasks and making assessments accordingly. But remember to build in an allowance for down-time such as travelling, movement between one location and another, and the sheer logistics of report preparation. Equally, your client may expect you and your team to all attend regular progress meetings and whilst you may be prepared to work until 3 a.m. to finish a report, will your secretary?

Delivery to budget

When the economy is in recession many organisations will not hire consultants at all. Of those who do, value for money will be a key issue, and invoices which indicate cost-overruns will get an understandably cold reception. A project may go over budget for a number of reasons. They include:

- under-budgeting key activities,
- poor time management,
- poor financial control.

Under-budgeting key activities

As noted earlier a poor workplan can result in late delivery. It may also mean extra resources have to be deployed to finish a task on schedule, if interdependent activities are not to be delayed. Consultants have a choice here: they can explain the problem to their client and discuss the impact on their fees, or they can absorb the costs themselves. If the situation has been caused by the client not honouring their part of the agreement, the situation may be amicably settled. However, passing on costs to your client in the hope that they will not be spotted is an unprofessional act which no legitimate consultant would contemplate.

Poor time management

If you are working with a team a related issue is the way in which you arrange the time of your colleagues. Whilst it may take an experienced consultant x hours to draft an opinion survey, a more junior colleague may take substantially longer. Consequently, your planning and project management needs to take account not only of the tasks being undertaken, but the calibre and experience of the consultant undertaking them. This is probably one of the most frustrating areas for the project manager, exemplified by the common comment: 'if only they were to do the task at my speed we would not be in this mess'.

It would be unfair to ascribe time management problems to your team members alone. All of us need to review our own working practices and preferred style. You may find your answers to the following provide some pointers to whether you are quite the paragon you imagine.

- do you have a plan for each day?
  - is it written down?
  - how do you prioritise your activities?
- looking back at yesterday
  - were you doing the right job at the right time?
  - could it have been done later?
  - could it have been delegated? To whom?

- how do you manage interruptions?
  - do they throw you off track?
  - how many interrupted tasks were left unfinished at the end of the day?

What is crucial as an internal consultant is to be able to track where the time went – the more so if you have a team working with you. Some form of time recording is essential if you are to justify your efforts to your client.

Poor financial control

At each step of the project expenditure and costs need to be monitored. This is particularly important if you are buying in services, whether they be software support or typing. It is absolutely critical that you set up systems and procedures to track all costs and expenditure.

MANAGING STAFF ENGAGED ON THE PROJECT

A consulting project has a whole raft of interdependencies and relationships. On many occasions you may be managing other consultants. We explore below the major aspects of this significant area of project management:

- the qualities good consultants possess and the implications this poses for the project manager,
- the categories of staff you may find yourself managing,
- the sorts of 'people problems' that can arise during a project and how to overcome them.

Key qualities

The following are some of the key qualities consultants need to possess:

The ability to think, analyse, diagnose and synthesise

Consulting requires the application of substantial 'brain power' at all stages of a project's life cycle. However, to choose individuals for their cerebral skills alone would run the very real risk of 'analysis paralysis'. What you do need are people who can quickly determine the key issues impacting on a situation and apply their diagnostic skills in a thoughtful yet incisive manner.

Honesty and integrity

In all their dealings with clients and colleagues consultants need to behave with impeccable integrity. At times they will be in possession of information which if abused or mishandled could cause substantial losses in both revenue and jobs. Preserving the confidentiality of this information and never placing themselves in a conflict of interests situation is of paramount importance. What is also important in a day-to-day sense is honesty. If you don't know you should say so. Bluffers in the consultancy profession are a liability to themselves, their colleagues and their clients.

Self-awareness

Consultancy is something of a pressure cooker with most things you do subject to review by colleagues, clients and not least yourself. One key area where this applies is in the area of 'consultant know thyself'. Without this quality and the confidence it brings to recognising learning opportunities, a consultant may find it difficult to operate at the highest level. They may also find it difficult to handle the pressures consulting can bring.

Interpersonal skills

The ability to relate to others is a key quality, whether during the sales process, managing a difficult meeting, or generating commitment to implement a project's recommendations. Top class consultants have high quality communication skills – both oral and written. They are also able to generate a vision of what success looks like, both to engage the interest of their client and to enthuse their team. This is a key area for the internal consultant, where demonstrating the need for change may well require substantial influencing skills.

A genuine desire to teach, train and help others learn, and to learn oneself

A key theme in contemporary consulting is the transfer of knowledge and skill from consultant to client organisation. One of the 'x' factors that differentiates an adequate consultant from an outstanding one is this quality. It revolves around an individual's capacity for self-learning and also their interest in challenging existing paradigms. Just as it was once observed that 'the future ain't what it used to be', the notion that a consultant can survive and prosper by hanging onto expert power has become redundant. For the internal consultant this may pose a very real challenge: how much to challenge current orthodoxy within the organisation? Here the need is to empower oneself to do just this.

Enthusiasm and tenacity

Without the persistence to follow an idea through or to have the tenacity to dig deeper to follow the workings of a process or procedure a consultant is unlikely to be successful.

Aside from professional rigour there must also be enthusiasm. An approach which is totally lacking in humanity or humour is not of itself sufficient. Both enthusiasm and tenacity will be required in large measure by the internal consultant. However, individuals with these skills will not always be the easiest to manage.

Implications for the project manager

Having explored the key qualities consultants (and their bosses) require, what are they likely to want from their manager? The following is one large consultancy's view:

- support at a working level. Here a key issue is the ability to understand the context within which the work is being undertaken and to relay this to the consultant. This aspect also raises the issue of whether, on a large project, the manager can actually be expected to be able to perform all of the tasks being undertaken by the consultant. As a manager you must put yourself in the shoes of your team members.
- guidance: help when asked for. Effective management consulting is about involvement and being sensitive to the needs of the individual. Sometimes a consulting project will be very similar to something a consultant has done before and well within their professional competence. On other occasions the process of diagnosis will test the consultant's skills to the maximum. As the project manager you need to create the time to be creative: i.e. to ensure yourself and colleagues do from time to time take a step back from the project and ask yourselves 'what if'. And even if someone is working on a project very similar to one they worked on in a line capacity this is not the same as working on it as a consultant. Many people enter consultancy from senior line roles where there is a considerable level of support and teamwork. Against this backdrop an individual's first job as a consultant can appear very lonely and exposed. You need to be aware of this and help people adjust to their new role.
- control: regular progress meetings. We all like to feel we know what's going on. Just as you will wish to keep your client informed of progress, so will you need to keep the team in touch with the 'big picture'.
- quality control. You need to ensure and assure the quality of the work being done.

All of this has implications for the way in which you manage your time, and you need to continually ask yourself if you are spending the right amount of time on cach of these four important areas.

Who might you be managing

Over time you may find yourself managing a wider range of individuals than you expected at the outset of your career. They will include:

Less experienced or more junior team members

These may be people whom you have handpicked as your unit develops its market. As noted above it is particularly important to recognise the significance of the first project. Paradoxically this may be more alarming to someone new to consulting, but with considerable line experience – after all, they will know what can go wrong. A more junior colleague on the other hand may lack some of the political sensitivities. So both types require you to act as a coach: to be available – on a daily basis if necessary – to 'play back' the events of the day and discuss progress. You will need to work on a development plan for each individual to ensure that where possible they 'learn by doing', but in a controlled environment. What this covers very much depends on the experience of the individual and the project in question. As an example, a consultant in their mid-20s might have limited experience of chairing meetings, so give them opportunities to run team progress meetings.

One area you need to consider is the risk of an inexperienced consultant 'going native'. Of its very nature consultancy provides opportunities to gain a rare insight into the challenges and constraints affecting an organisation. Quite junior consultants may find themselves included in strategic discussions about future corporate policies. On occasion an individual consultant may feel very real sympathy for a particular proposition or the stand taken by a key individual. Indeed, they may end a project with a much warmer working relationship with their client than they have ever experienced with their boss! There is nothing wrong with this, but at all times consultants must be mindful of the reason for their involvement – to provide impartial, objective, professional advice; You simply can't do this if you take sides. This aspect should not be confused with reading the politics of an organisation. As a consultant you will frequently be in positions where your antennae need to be on full power.

'Experts'

Some older consultants may yearn for the days when it was possible to be a 'jack of all trades'. The reality of today's marketplace is somewhat different and you may well find yourself managing a team which includes people with expert skills in a discipline other than your own. Depending on the nature of your internal consulting unit these individuals may be full-time members of your team or freelance consultants hired in by you because of their specific expertise.

As the person responsible to the client for the delivery of the project you must ensure that you fully understand what is going to be done by your 'expert' to produce the final result. For example, if the project involves computer modelling you need to go through the tasks involved in detail and second-guess any areas where work may get off-track. This needs to happen before the project starts if at all possible. You will also need to clarify the nature of the relationship with the client. It will not do your credibility any good if your 'expert' decides on their own initiative to brief senior management on progress. Just as the project has terms of reference so will these members of your team need guidelines on what's expected.

Client counterpart staff

Increasingly – and quite rightly – clients are looking to consulting projects to result in a transfer of knowledge and skills from the consultant into the organisation. For this reason many projects now include client counterpart staff who will work alongside the team and gain experience which they can take back to the workplace. In theory such an arrangement sounds beneficial to everyone. The reality can be a nightmare for the project manager. This generally focuses around two issues; the calibre of the counterpart and the time they have available. You need to draw up a detailed specification of the type of individual required and the skills and abilities they must already possess, or your client may seriously underestimate the level of learning transfer which will take place from consultant to counterpart. If this does happen your client will almost certainly ascribe the failure to 'those consultants', rather than a poor choice of counterpart. Without a clear person specification all sorts of things may go wrong. You may find yourself given a manager who has expressed a desire to learn more about IT for career development reasons, but with no IT experience, assigned as the link man in a review of IT strategy. You may be given someone whom it is deemed 'needs to improve their interpersonal skills'. So you need to build into your proposal your own involvement in the choice of counterparts. Your proposal must also have made clear what the time commitment of a counterpart is and at what stage in the project they will be required. The authors have experience of one project where the counterpart was consistently promised by the client but only made an appearance in the last quarter of the work. By this time those aspects of the project which would have developed the required in-house expertise for progress to be sustained after the consultants' departure, had largely been concluded.

Line staff

For part of a project you may have line staff seconded to you, perhaps as technical advisers or to provide technical support. Despite your best efforts such individuals may not be very clear about the purpose of the project. Indeed they may be extremely suspicious about their involvement in it. It is important that you establish at the outset what the 'game rules' of their involvement are to be, where their contribution fits into the overall plan, and any sensitivities specific to the project. Neither should the individual's boss be forgotten – they may be seething that their 'key man' has been removed at a moment's notice to assist with a project about which they know nothing.

Building and managing a team

If your people do not know what is expected of them problems may occur. Two key aspects of your role will therefore be giving feedback and acting as a coach.

Giving feedback

Irrespective of the category of staff involved in your project you need to establish a means of giving feedback. For those working with you on a regular basis it is important that you set aside the time to discuss progress not on a project basis but from the individual's perspective. The frequency of such meetings depends on the duration of the project, but as a rule of thumb a monthly meeting would seem sensible. By focusing on how the individual 'sees things going' you will get an invaluable insight into the project; its strengths, weaknesses, successes and failures through their eyes. At the end of the project a more formal review needs to take place where learning points can be discussed and agreed. At this stage it is valuable to review both the 'what' and the 'how' of the project. Thus, were deadlines achieved, but at the expense of alienating client staff? You may find it helpful to consider the qualities discussed on page 95 and build these into the discussion. If you are to do this you will need to be able to provide behavioural evidence in support of your comments. In other words how had the consultant's approach 'shown up' to yourself and the client. A possible framework for a straightforward non-bureaucratic review document is shown in Fig. 4.1.

Feedback to staff not directly under your control may take a number of routes, for example via a counterpart's own boss. In all cases it is important that there has been prior agreement as to what is expected and the level of performance anticipated.

Coaching

Coaching may best be defined as the provision of help to a colleague through direct discussion and guided activity to learn how to solve a problem or enhance performance within a job. It may be provided by you but could possibly be provided by another person with the relevant knowledge or skills. Coaching could include working with a consultant to encourage them to take on a new task which extends their job scope and provides experience in a new area. Another opportunity would be to let the consultant run a client meeting normally chaired by yourself.

Project:	Describe the nature of the work undertaken, specify the tasks for which the consultant was responsible and review effectiveness
Performance (WHAT):	Describe consultant performance against key tasks – did they deliver what was required? On time? In the right way? One way to review this aspect is to use the workplan and discuss any overruns or additions which impacted on the consultant or were caused by the consultant's performance

Performance (HOW):

Analysis, Synthesis

Interpersonal skills

Enthusiasm

Self-awareness

Honesty and integrity

Development needs: review with the consultant what learning has emerged from the project and jointly determine what you both need to do next and the timescale

Fig. 4.1 Sample consultant review document

Of course, delegating some of your responsibilities could represent risk to yourself. However, if you do not delegate worthwhile tasks your team members will not learn.

One way of thinking about the coaching process is that it is akin to an athlete being helped to 'lift the bar' to a personal best performance. It is very much about encouraging an individual to feel that they can make a difference. However, all too often the potential which effective coaching should release is blocked. Take the following example: a consultant in your team comes to talk to you about how to develop an internal client relationship. Your instant response is along the lines of 'you need to do this, then . . .' etc. What you should aim for is to get the consultant to identify the problems they may encounter in developing the relationship and how they think they could overcome these. Your intervention should be along the lines of encouraging the consultant to think of what else they could try and to make yourself available subsequently to review with them progress and barriers to achievement. The difference is between that of directing – 'do it my way and it will be OK' – and guiding: 'how might they react if you suggest that to them?'

'Chemistry'

However cohesive and well managed the team, on rare occasions a consultant does not 'click' with the client. This can happen at the proposal stage or during the exercise itself. And it can and does happen to very good consultants. Careful matching of what the job requires with the consultant's expertise can certainly minimise the risk, as can the approach of 'what you see is what you get'. In other words the team that presents the proposal is the team that will actually do the work.

Should this situation happen with someone working for you, there are two key concerns: to establish the precise cause of client displeasure, and then to take appropriate action. Issues of performance are dealt with below. If the concern is more with 'fit' with the project, then you may well need to remove the consultant. However, what you do afterwards is crucial. A large consulting practice would be concerned to ensure the consultant learned from the experience and that their confidence was not destroyed by the episode. Indeed the author once managed an exercise where the client decided one of the team lacked the necessary 'oomph' to deliver a training programme. They were duly removed. This did not prevent them being acceptable as a provider of a different service to the same client some months later.

What you must consider as an internal consultant is the impact of one of your team being declared '*persona non grata*'. The lesson here would seem to be to take great care over the selection of your team and to involve a cross-section of senior potential clients in the selection process.

OBTAINING FEEDBACK FROM THE CLIENT AND TESTING CLIENT SATISFACTION

Here we should distinguish your individual client to whom you may be reporting, and the client organisation within which you are working. Apart from the 'client' other individuals and groups will be useful sources of feedback, namely:

- the project manager,
- client staff,
- senior management,
- 'others in the organisation who see what you are doing'.

Once again there are a variety of ways in which you get feedback from these individuals and groups. Inevitably it may be easier to get feedback from your client, given the nature of the working relationship. With, say, senior management, there is a need throughout the project to tap their feelings on 'how it's going', but you also from time to time need to elicit views on key aspects of the project. The following are the key themes:

- adherence to terms of reference,
- the extent to which results met expectations,
- whether the benefits delivered were greater or lesser than anticipated,
- the quality and usefulness of presentations,

- adherence to the project schedule,
- any surprises in fee/invoice amounts,
- the extent to which the consultants understood client requirements and demonstrated this,
- the ease with which any unexpected problems or deviations from the schedule were handled,
- learning points for the consultants'
- how well did the consultants manage their relationship with client staff,
- the frequency and usefulness of progress meetings,
- speed of response to client enquiries and access to consultants when required.

For professionals who are allegedly well versed in fact-finding techniques, consultants are sometimes surprisingly naive about getting feedback from their client. In part this may be explained by a quite proper concern with getting the job done. However, whilst a task orientation is a necessity, so is a concern with relationship management. Most human beings are concerned to be in control of events – your clients will be no exception to this. So what do you need to do?

Acknowledge the client's perspective

There are a range of concerns that we all experience as customers. Most frustrating of all is to complain, be listened to and find that your provider – estate agent, garage, or consultant – does absolutely nothing to rectify the situation. Regular meetings, informal lunches, and contact during the project can all help you keep in touch. As a result of such contact it is far better, if you realise there is a problem, to openly acknowledge it to your client. In the long run this is much more likely to strengthen your relationship. Silence may well destroy it.

As far as your client is concerned they can never get enough attention. They will soon let you know if they have no time. However, if **you** don't create the time to establish a good working relationship you will not be in a position to get the feedback so important for success. Think about the relationship through your client's eyes. The project upon which you are about to embark may represent the result of years of lobbying by your client. It may represent considerable risk to their career should it fail. Whilst a consultant may view each project dispassionately, for your client it may be a significant act of faith.

Think about the organisation's experience with consultants. Most of us have come up against cynicism at some point during most projects. Ask yourself what the project really represents to your client and you will recognise the following as important determinants of your success.

Effective communication throughout the project

Effective communication recurs as a theme throughout this book, suffice to say here that a consultant can never overestimate its importance.

Continuity

If your project requires a team, recognise that frequent changes in team composition can be unsettling for your client unless you very clearly signal at the start of the project that your *modus operandi* is to use specialists for discrete areas of the work. The explanation that 'something else came up' is both unprofessional and unacceptable. There must be a reference point for the client in the form of the project manager.

An understanding of business issues

As an internal consultant you should have a major strength – you know the business. But what you must also be able to demonstrate is a knowledge of business practice in similar sectors, industries or technologies. This understanding is something that should not just be brought out in your final report. During a project there will be many opportunities to show your expertise. However, beware of the trap of arrogance. The key skill is to be able to deploy your knowledge in a manner which enhances your professional competence without antagonising those around you.

From the client's perspective the assistance you are providing is **the** most important thing. Your client will react with extreme displeasure if they feel you are juggling them with another client.

Give your client feedback!

A genuine professional relationship needs to be two-way. If your client is not providing the time the project requires you must diplomatically point this out.

MONITORING AND MEASURING PROGRESS TOWARDS OBJECTIVES

As with any project a consultancy exercise requires vigilance and care if it is to achieve the desired result. In essence this means hard work and adherence to a consistent approach. Many internal consultants will be well versed in project management techniques and may have used software systems to manage themselves and their projects. Others may be new to the discipline required. Whatever your experience you need to be clear about the importance of a clear workplan.

The workplan

A maxim consultants would do well to remember is that you cannot manage what you cannot measure. Consequently, a great deal of consideration needs to go into the development of your workplan. One way of thinking about the workplan is as a bridge between the terms of reference and the practical conduct of the project. A properly constructed workplan can reduce the impact of many of the potential problems identified in this chapter, namely:

- ensuring delivery on time and on budget,
- achieving the optimum fit between the consultants and the tasks

making up the project, by identifying the interdependencies in the project and an appropriate sequence of tasks.

Developing a plan cannot be conducted in isolation from your client as the following steps show:

Purpose

When your proposal was presented and accepted there may have been a rosy glow of clarity and confidence. However, some time may have elapsed since the acceptance and your client will no doubt have been grappling with a wide range of other business issues. So begin by doing three things:

- go back to the proposed terms of reference and reflect on whether the project is focused on diagnosis and/or proposing solutions.
- reflect to your client your precise understanding of what the project involves. It is essential that any gap between what you are proposing to deliver and that which your client is expecting, is explored at this stage.
- following on from this you must specify what shape the project deliverables will take.

Task identification

Your plan will be a working document. As such it should specify what needs to happen, by when, and how you will recognise when a particular task has been completed.

To take an example, an analysis of the market in which your organisation operates might include the activities and deliverables shown in Table 4.1.

This would be broken down into more detailed steps and a timetable created, as shown in Fig. 4.2.

In positioning the activities into the timetable remember to include client activities in the workplan. In the example shown above you would need to clarify with the client what information currently exists upon which to identify customers to be interviewed. Be wary of a response which runs along the lines of 'I'm sure we'll be able to

Activities	Deliverables
• analyse structure of the industry • analyse size and geography of markets • examine future market scenarios • design customer interview questionnaire • conduct interviews • analyse interviews	• develop customer needs profile • model of current and future market trends • segmentation of types of customer

Table 4.1 Sample deliverable in a market analysis project

Activities\Month	M	A	M	J	J	A	S	O	N	D
Design customer interviews	→→									
Identity interviewees		→→								
Set/undertake interviews			→→							
Conduct interview analysis				→→						

Fig. 4.2 Sample project timetable

provide the information when the time comes'. Invariably this expectation remains unfulfilled.

Monitor and revise your plans

Your workplan will provide a visible and tangible means of assessing progress. However, it remains a plan not a strait-jacket. It is important that you explain to your client at the start of the project that you will continuously monitor progress and that some revision may be

PROGRESS SHEET			
Key Tasks	Due by	Complete/Incomplete	Factors affecting completion

Fig. 4.3 Sample progress sheet

necessary. In other words, the plan is based on your current knowledge of the situation.

Progress meetings

As we note throughout this book progress meetings are essential. Apart from meetings with your client you will need regular meetings of your team. It is a good idea to give each consultant a specific progress sheet relating to the tasks they will be undertaking and to use this to update each other at your meetings. An example sheet is shown in Fig. 4.3.

This gets people to focus on what has or has not been completed and will give you a straightforward means of spotting bottlenecks or areas where progress has been speedier than anticipated.

SPOTTING OPPORTUNITIES TO SELL ON

The Personnel Director of a large insurance company commented 'I hate management consultants'. Professional curiosity aroused, we probed further. Key concerns were:

- that consultants should be used selectively or judiciously otherwise 'they take over and create an agenda of their own making, not mine'; and
- they continuously look out for opportunities to 'sell something else'.

Now, whether or not management consultants like this image, there is no doubt that it is a very real perception. Indeed, a recent experience of the author's reinforces it: at a recent meeting of a prestigious dinner club there were eight consultants from one well-known consultancy. Ambulance chasing it would appear is alive and well in the consultancy profession! So, how is the internal consultant to avoid this charge? Fortunately, there are a number of ways of so doing:

Positioning yourself at the outset of the project

A key issue here is what kind of consultant you are presenting yourself as. Thus, if you are a sole practitioner offering internal consultancy in, say, Total Quality Management (TQM), your clients may be surprised that you subsequently offer to provide assistance on process re-engineering the business. On the other hand, in a large organisation there may well be a network of internal consultants with a wide range of expertise and this capability can be referred to in your original proposal. At the conclusion of the project you can identify issues emerging which go beyond the scope of the current exercise and suggest ways in which they might be tackled. A common frustration for consultants who have completed a successful project is to be told by their client some months later that another consultancy has been engaged for a new project; 'we didn't ask you to pitch because we didn't know you could do it!' This is less likely in the context of internal consultancy. More likely is a view that an internal consultant lacks the credibility or capability to undertake a particular project or lacks the objective impartiality to tackle it. Overcoming this barrier takes time. It requires continuous internal marketing, appropriate networking, and a track record of demonstrable success.

Maintain regular contact with your client

No consultancy project can be performed without this. But distinguish between the regular and vital meetings so important for effective project management and wider blue sky meetings on 'what if'. Some clients will tell you quite firmly that their only concern is the project in hand. Others will be interested – the more so if you share your thoughts on developments elsewhere. It is a continuing surprise to many management consultants that their clients are not better versed in what's happening in their own marketplace. But they are not – and this presents you with a major opportunity to demonstrate your expertise. So if you spot an article in a trade journal or the professional press which you know will be of interest to your client, send them a copy.

Don't make assumptions

Despite the alleged clarity of their thought processes, consultants are sometimes apparently unaware of a new project opportunity very obvious to a rival consultancy. So from time to time take off your project management blinkers and ask yourself the question 'if I were the client what would my next major challenge be?'

Network

Networking has entered the management vocabulary in recent years. In fact effective consultants have been practising it for much longer – they have had no choice. You must continually think about opportunities for others to learn of your skills and equally to learn from others of new approaches and opportunities. In the internal context, a satisfied client who can be persuaded to host a lunch for, say, Divisional MD's or participate in a workshop on what your internal consultancy service can offer, is invaluable. In large organisations internal consultancy teams will frequently use techniques like these. In a smaller business a more informal approach may be required.

Some of the key aspects of the 'selling on' process are explained below. They focus on identifying the signals that an opportunity exists, what the opportunities may be, and for whom.

What are the signals?

If you are particularly fortunate client behaviour will send you a strong signal; they will ask you how you might approach a particular problem. In other cases the client will make a point of offering to recommend you to other colleagues.

What are the opportunities?

Opportunities can come in a number of guises. They may be new work with your existing client or new work with a 'new' client. In the internal context this could be another department or division.

Equally the opportunity may take the form of additional work for yourself or another consultant in your unit. It might also be for someone else entirely. You shouldn't be afraid of identifying a need that **you** cannot meet, but which another consultant can.

SPOTTING DANGER SIGNALS

So far this chapter has examined what effective internal consultants need to do to 'achieve'. We have seen there are numerous pressure points that can derail or slow down the most carefully prepared plan. Monitoring and measuring progress towards objectives can remove many 'risks'. However, danger signals may emerge from the following:

- the client;
- the project team;
- changes outside the project.

In each case the need is to be sensitive to the signals which are being sent and to develop an appropriate response to them.

The client

This may take a number of forms ranging from direct criticism about a specific issue, such as a consultant failing to show up at a meeting; to comments of a more indirect nature, for example repeated requests for assurances that the project 'is still on track'. If direct criticism is warranted, you obviously need to be seen to take action. More oblique comments may point to a need for communication rather than action, so you need to be able to show that things are on track, but you also need to check out why the client is concerned.

A signal which is more difficult to counteract is a waning of interest on the part of your client. Should this be the case – and it may be exemplified by the client sending a deputy to meetings for example – you need to explain to your client the significance of their involvement in the project and the impact that any lessening of their support will have.

The project team

Stresses and strains will always occur in project teams and good project management can enable a disparate mix of individuals to share a common vision of what the project entails. However, sometimes cracks do appear. They may show through in the form of missed deadlines, poor quality work, grumbling about the workplan, or rows between colleagues. The key challenge for the project manager is to very quickly discover what the cause is and reassert their authority.

Changes outside the project

Of its very nature consultancy is about the successful management of change. Although not every project is a large-scale programme integrated with strategic business plans, any project may fall victim of the very change process of which it is part. Changes in Board membership or a change in business direction may create a situation in which your project is untenable. In these circumstances you need to review the situation with your client and determine whether the project should continue, pause for an agreed period, or in extreme circumstances be aborted.

Using your antennae

Inevitably, many problems do not always appear in a readily

compartmentalised manner. So the message here is: constantly review your project in your mind, muse over how things are going. Apart from your workplan you could find it helpful to keep a daily log in which to record your feelings about progress and aspects of the project that you believe may require extra effort. The log will help you during the project as a simple 'memory jogger'. At the conclusion of the exercise it will also provide you with a valuable learning tool against which to review how you planned things to happen and what actually occurred.

5

THE FIVE SECRETS OF SUCCESSFUL IMPLEMENTATION

This chapter reviews those aspects critical to successful implementation:

- effective communication;
- managing progress meetings;
- presenting results and delivering reports that have impact;
- influencing tactics;
- cost and benefit analysis of recommendations.

Ensuring recommendations are acted upon and that the consulting project 'bears fruit' requires a number of skills, not least considerable energy and personal organisation. Implementation is very much about change and without effective communication an implementation plan which looks great on paper may be doomed. Equally as a consultant you need both the presentational skills to persuade your audience of the benefits of your proposition and the ability to produce reports which have impact. The ability to influence your client throughout the project may also make considerable demands upon you. A key facet in this context can be the role you play in the successful conduct of progress meetings.

EFFECTIVE COMMUNICATION

In any organisation communication takes place on a variety of levels both formal and informal, verbal and written. As a consultant you need to be aware of the impact of all forms of communication and harness the most appropriate means to get maximum impact. This may not be as straightforward as you would think as the following example shows:

Company A decided to conduct an examination of opportunities for business process redesign. There was significant debate between the company and their chosen consultants about the need for regular communication, both with the top team and the staff in general. To facilitate this, a steering group was set up to meet at regular intervals to discuss progress. The consultants determined that this was not necessary in the short term and decided to brief senior managers individually rather than collectively.

This resulted in a number of disaffected senior managers feeling disempowered by the process and suspecting that they were receiving partial feedback. Their trust in the consultancy team diminished. Realising this the consultants quickly made clear to everyone that one-to-one discussions enabled more detailed discussion to take place so in a real sense they were getting **more** *information. In addition, presentations to the whole management team were scheduled to enable the group as a whole to review progress.*

Do not forget the importance of communication before the project has started. How will staff and line managers learn about it? Do trade unions need to be briefed. And by whom? Is there a company newspaper? Do special meetings need to be convened? Who is responsible for signing off any communications? A real problem here may be that in an organisation about to attempt to undergo culture change existing channels of communication may be very poor. The author, some years ago, arrived at a company's premises to conduct an attitude survey and during a focus group 'discovered' that the participants had turned up the previous day having been given the wrong information by their managers. It appeared this was not an unusual situation.

Establish yardsticks

To guide you, think very clearly about:

- what needs to be communicated;
- by whom;
- by when;
- and by what means.

In practice this raises two areas requiring action. The first relates to 'fitness for purpose', in other words choosing the most appropriate technique. A number of these are dealt with in this chapter. The second is how you as an individual communicate. Here we need to return to the characteristics of effective consultants, in particular the need for honesty and integrity.

As an internal consultant you will frequently be placed in situations where you will need to manage the balance between being open about the nature and purpose of your project and absolute discretion about your findings and recommendations. Thus the more you encourage people to be open and honest with you the more they are likely to ask what you think of the current situation. In these circumstances musing out loud is dangerous. Within hours you find that the most effective informal communications channel of all – the grapevine – is telling the workforce 'the consultant thinks . . .'.

Delivering presentations

Presentations are a key element in successful consulting – whether to sell a job, present results or gain commitment to proceed with implementation. However, getting them right is not easy and most of us have seen consultants who, whilst technically excellent, are very poor communicators. Once upon a time this may not have mattered, today it is a key consideration. Consultancy long ago emerged from that of a shadow profession judged on the quality of reports. Now the emphasis is exactly the same as that for senior management – communication is a key competency. It may be helpful to take a look at some of the key components:

influence – the ability to persuade people using appropriate influencing styles;

impact – having the self-confidence to enable others to clearly see your position and the ability to project yourself in a variety of situations;

clarity – the ability to present ideas clearly so that others quickly understand what is being communicated.

Just as during a consulting project it is essential to establish rapport with your client, so is there a need when presenting to come across as clear, professional and **interesting.** It may be a truism to suggest that 'I'll believe it when I see it, and I'll see it when I believe it' but it is important that a consultant demonstrates confidence and belief in that which they are proposing or recommending. They need to be able to relate to the needs of their audience and think about how they can illustrate both their experience of making things happen and their understanding of the client's situation.

Confidence should not be confused with complacency. A first-rate consultancy project can be seriously threatened by a presentation that 'goes wrong' because of a failure to rehearse. Large consultancies are arguably likely to have more problems with this – for example a Partner delivering the results of a survey without a full knowledge of the background to it. This issue can of course be easily resolved by getting the consultants who did the work involved in the presentation. What is much more damaging is for the information presented to be flawed and challenged as such by the audience. For example the author was once presented with a 'fact' which related to the level of market salaries in his own organisation allegedly being seriously adrift to those of a major competitor. Upon challenging this it became clear that what was being quoted was anecdotal evidence from one individual. The consequence was to raise concern about the accuracy of other data. Equally damaging to the credibility of the presenter are flaws such as the incorrect spelling of the Chief Executive's name: avoid this at all costs.

We explore below the steps you can take to correctly position your presentation and get maximum benefit from it.

Why do we do presentations?

A presentation has a number of advantages:

- it is interactive and enables you to gauge opinions and reactions on the spot;
- it is time effective by gathering together a number of relevant people at the same time;
- it enables you to choose the focus and concentrate on what you think is important, and;
- it gives you the opportunity to use your skills of persuasion to obtain the outcome you desire.

There are some disadvantages however. In particular:

- there is a limit to the detail you can give and the amount your audience will be able to absorb through a presentation alone;
- the time available may be insufficient for the breadth and depth of the information you are conveying.

When we do presentations for clients, we may be looking for a range of outcomes. If we are *informing*, we may:

- summarise findings and present conclusions;
- explain how much work we have done to date (for example a progress report);
- make sure the client understands the consequences of recommendations and difficulties that could arise during implementation.

If, on the other hand, we are attempting to *persuade*, we may wish to:

- gain acceptance for ideas;
- seek agreement;
- get a decision;
- sell further work.

Planning your presentation

As in all aspects of consultancy, planning is essential. In planning a presentation you must:

- set the objectives of the presentation;
- understand the needs of the audience;
- structure your presentation;
- ensure that you get the timing right;
- use visual aids effectively and consider how to present figures.
- consider your body language;
- rehearse and test out your responses to anticipated questions.

Objectives

The outcome of your presentation must be clear in your own mind, but clarify it with your client as well. For example, your client may want to use the opportunity of having the top 100 managers in the business together at one time to sow the seeds of future strategy. You may therefore be asked to structure your approach accordingly.

Audience

Your strategy will depend on your audience. Who are they? What are their needs? The internal consultant should have an advantage here in so far as many attendees may be personally known to you. However you must consider the relationships between the people in your audience:

- is there likely to be opposition? If so, who will handle it – yourself or your client?

- if different people in the audience have different levels of under-standing, who do you address? If you have any concern whatsoever about this check it out before the presentation, or if this is impossible, at the beginning. It is far better to risk minor embarrassment by this enquiry than waste two hours of valuable time telling people what they already know, or talking over their heads.
- is there conflict between members of the audience? What impact will this have on atmosphere? Will it show through in the questions asked?

Structure

Getting the structure of your presentation right is the single most important thing you can do after setting your objectives. The following sequence will help you:

- identify the key themes and major points you need to cover. Use cards or flipcharts to capture them.
- decide upon the sequence in which they should be presented.
- build on this by amplifying the material. At this point you must return to your objective and the audience. An overview of progress on a quality assurance project may require a limited number of graphs. A presentation to line managers on inventory control problems and proposed solutions might require much more detailed statistical analysis.
- in the light of the time you have available practise the presentation and adjust the content as necessary.
- prepare an introduction to 'set the scene'.
- check the acoustics. Will you need a microphone?
- check the seating. Will everybody be able to see you?
- is there a clock?
- if you are presenting from a podium what will you do with your notes? Will there be enough light to read them?
- prepare a summary which reflects your objective, e.g. milestones reached, work outstanding, benefits of your approach.

Timing

Everyone overruns. Allow for the actual presentation to take up to 50 per cent longer to give than it takes you to rehearse it. That allows for questions, time spent handling visual aids, and unforeseen events. Also, consider the 'best' time to make a presentation. Nine o'clock on a Monday morning may mean many people in your audience will be preoccupied by the week ahead.

Visual aids

Remember, if your audience sees a picture of what you are talking about, they retain significantly more information than if they simply hear about it.

Visual aids:

- guide your audience through the talk;
- help them see the structure;
- show material visually that would otherwise be difficult to grasp.

To do this you need to:

- introduce the visual before you pick it up;
- give yourself time to make the important point which almost always precedes a visual, and to let it sink in;
- show the visual;
- check that they can all see; if not, invite them to move. Give them a very rapid summary of how the visual is designed:

  e.g. *the red areas show trends . . .*
  the horizontal axis relates to market share . . .

  Then keep quiet while they take it in. If they still can't get the message from it at this point, it's too complex. Watch their eyes, not the visual, to gauge their reaction, and to know when to start talking again.
- focus their attention. When about half of the audience turn back to you, remind them again why you are showing it and go into detail.

Presenting figures

The lively presentation of figures is a challenging task for any presenter. Most consulting projects require it at some point. To do so effectively requires consideration of the following:

- *What do they want to do with the information?* Senior people are not necessarily number-crunchers, and don't want to have to do the analysis for themselves. You have to offer a view of what is significant, to focus their eyes and minds. Don't assume that the figures speak for themselves: it is your job to make them speak.
- *How much information do they need?* Only provide as much as will help your audience understand your message or make a decision,

no more. If they ask for details, have them ready, but be aware that they illustrate a message: they are not the message itself.

- *How accurate does it need to be*? How accurate was the means by which it was collected? To be accurate to the nearest pound on the balance sheet, when the inventories were only accurate to the nearest £1,000, may be misleading.
- *How can you help them assimilate it*?
  – Choose memorable, strong shapes to show trends and connections only. Details are difficult to read precisely.
  – Approximate and simplify. You can give exact figures in handouts. Highlight the most significant ideas and patterns with a verbal summary.

Technology

Software packages now allow slides to be produced which are visually very exciting. However, do not be seduced by the technology available to you. Using a flipchart during your presentation may be far more compelling than an over-busy slide. You would also be unwise to use a computer linked projector to create a slide show unless you are very familiar with the technology. For a presentation to more than 40 people 35mm slides are a better bet They will come across much more clearly than overhead slides. For a smaller group overhead slides will allow you considerably more interaction with the audience.

Do ensure you are familiar with the venue in which the presentation will be given. Do not choose the technology before you see the surroundings.

Body language

How you appear will send some powerful signals to your audience. We identify below some key aspects that differentiate an assured, confident presentation from an awkward rambling discourse. Everyone has mannerisms. They only become comic or irritating when they are accentuated by nervousness and you are not aware of them. If you know what you tend to do, you are in a position to stop.

Voice:

- talk to the back of the room;
- keep your voice up; don't let it drop at the end of the sentence;
- pause deliberately to allow significant points to sink in.

Face:

- keep your face moving and expressive;
- keep eye contact. Look at the bridge of their noses, not the ceiling, the floor or your visuals. Look at everyone, but watch out for the lighthouse effect where you continually scan the audience but never hold anyone's gaze. This will encourage your audience to believe you are not certain of your facts.

Body:

- you do not have to be rigid to be formal – move naturally;
- let your gestures and movements mirror the meaning of what you are saying;
- find a comfortable 'base' position to return to;
- do not be concerned about using space. A presenter who never comes out from behind their lectern – even for questions – is unlikely to get much rapport with their audience.

Handling questions

Think about what questions you might be asked and prepare answers to them. At this point think about whether it would be better to anticipate the questions by amending the presentation. Get colleagues to test you out by asking a variety of questions of you. As important as the content of your answer is the way you handle the question. Consultants can get too used to 'consultant speak' and become oblivious to the jargon they use. So ask questioners whether they feel you have actually answered the question. If you are involved in a team presentation it is imperative that there is prior agreement as to who will co-ordinate responses to questions. An eager consultant leaping in to answer a question to show off their expertise may undo all your efforts at presenting a proposition in a particular way.

Rehearsals

Rehearsals justify a separate mention for a number of reasons. Without them you cannot possibly prepare and deliver an effective presentation. But more than this, used in the right way they are an incredibly powerful learning tool, the more so if you use video to capture **what** you say and **how** you present it. Thus the only real way of learning about the signals your body language sends is to watch yourself. And as you do so ask – is that the way I want to come across? – and get feedback from your colleagues on whether what 'shows up' is an assured, confident presenter or someone who is glib and cocky or apparently disorganised and lacking in confidence.

How did you do?

Once you have prepared and rehearsed the presentation, imagine yourself amongst your audience, and rate yourself on the checklist below. Equally, use it on other people's presentations: what makes them clear and memorable, and why?

Drafting a presentation for someone else

From time to time it will be necessary for your client or sponsor to make presentations about the project, perhaps to gain commitment or to explain the ramifications of recommendations. On these occasions take nothing for granted: offer to prepare a draft presentation, walk the individual through it and if at all possible get them to rehearse it with you. Some senior executives get so enmeshed in a project that they forget the perspective of their audience. You cannot afford for this to happen.

Running workshops and focus groups

The techniques for fact-finding were dealt with earlier in this book. In the context of project management the need is to ensure that appropriate techniques are utilised and that their purpose is clearly demonstrated and communicated.

ASSESSMENT CHECKLIST

1. What was the speaker offering you?

2. What did the speaker want from you? Did they get it?

3. How much of the time did they hold your attention?

0%   50%   100%

Reasons:

Voice   Language

Body   Information

Visuals   Structure

4. What is the most vivid impression still in your mind?

Fig. 5.1 Presentation assessment checklist

Example: An organisation decided it needed a review of pay and grading arrangements. The management team accepted this need, a consultant was chosen and the fact that the review would be conducted was communicated in staff meetings, via E-Mail and the in-house journal. However, for a variety of reasons the review was delayed by some weeks. By the time groups of supervisors were convened to get their views on pay, memories had faded and there was concern about 'why this chap wants to talk to us' from both participants and their bosses. Continuously ask yourself: has the purpose been made clear?

Workshops and focus groups

During a project there may be a need to collect information, test out hypotheses and to train client staff in the use of a particular technique. Workshops and focus groups are valuable tools.

Focus groups

Focus groups are just what their name implies: a group of people gathered together to focus on a specific issue or theme. They can feature in a project at a variety of stages. Examples would be:

- a group of employees from a particular department convened at the outset of a project to get views from staff on current arrangements/processes;
- groups of employees convened after an attitude survey had been conducted to 'flesh out' the thinking and opinions underpinning the results;
- a group of supervisors/managers convened towards the end of a project to test out the impact of proposed changes to pay and grading arrangements.

Whatever the stage of the project, there are a number of factors to take into account:

Composition
Given that the purpose of focus groups is to elicit responses, the optimum number of participants should not exceed a dozen. The

segmentation of participants depends on the purpose, but you should avoid convening groups in which bosses and their subordinates participate. The presence of anyone 'senior' is likely to prevent participants expressing their true feelings. You will also need to make a decision on which parts of the organisation participants come from. Testing out overall impressions of morale may make a mix of participants from across the organisation the preferred approach. Where the objective is to test out something specific – IT effectiveness – for example, you might wish to convene different groups representing the user community and the providers.

Communication and confidentiality
As an internal consultant you must remind yourself that some individuals will see you as a potential stool pigeon reporting verbatim back to the Board. A few simple steps can help overcome participant reticence and concern:

- explain the context of the discussion. Emphasise that without open discussion and full information the project will not succeed. Guarantee to safeguard the confidentiality of information and the anonymity of respondents. Explain that if you were to break this rule you would soon lose your professional credibility.
- do however alert participants to the fact that should unexpected themes or concerns emerge you will feed these back to your client; **but without attribution.**
- participation should be voluntary: a personal letter of invitation from the MD and careful briefing of line managers can ensure commitment and interest from most people.

Running the focus group

The purpose of the focus group is to get information and it is important that the event is appropriately managed or it may turn into a grumble session about the organisation.

Example: an inexperienced consultant was pulled into a project at short notice, with little knowledge of the client. He was unsure of his ground and allowed the discussion to be dominated by two people who between them had substantial service with the company and very strong views about the nature of change within the business. Afterwards another participant sent the consultant her own thoughts on the topics discussed, having remained silent during the focus group: 'I didn't like to say anything the other day . . . they were so firm in their views . . . but they are not representative of the people I work with'.

The golden rules are:

- explain the structure and timing of the discussion. Start with open questions to get the group talking.
- get everyone to introduce themselves to each other – it helps break the ice.
- stay in control, be firm but fair. Your job is to give everyone a chance to contribute. At intervals throughout the discussion summarise views and go around the table individually checking agreement or disagreement. If someone is dominating the group ask them a factual question. When they answer, ask someone else what he or she thinks about the response. To draw out someone who is not taking an active part ask an interpretive question that requires a detailed response.
- stay neutral – you are not there to agree or disagree. One analogy is with an air traffic controller – your role is to co-ordinate a number of complex and often simultaneous streams of thought.
- record ideas. Depending on the circumstances you may wish to use a flipchart to record ideas or keep notes as you go along. If the latter is your choice think very seriously about having a colleague with you to act as 'scribe'. It is **very** difficult to facilitate and focus groups and make notes simultaneously.
- at the conclusion explain what next – i.e. what you will be doing with the information; when your report and recommendations will be presented.

Workshops

The purpose of workshops is somewhat different to the focus group. A workshop is more concerned with explaining how something may work and testing it out, or giving participants skills in, say, job

evaluation techniques to enable the next stage of a project to proceed. As such, a different range of skills are called for. Be aware that
not all consultants are good trainers, just as good trainers do not
necessarily make good consultants. Running a workshop may be a
completely new experience for a consultant and great care needs to
be taken in developing an approach that will actually work.

*Example: Consultants working on a major IT programme in the
banking sector needed to run workshops for key personnel on how the
new system would work. Their initial approach was heavily focused on
lectures 'to explain how to use the system'. They were concerned that
such an approach didn't 'feel right' and tested out their approach with a
colleague. The workshop which was subsequently developed
emphasised learning by doing, supported by a detailed operations
manual. This is an important distinction which reflects the nature of
learning: most effective is for us to observe an event or process taking
place and working out from that how we might go about doing it
ourselves. Merely reading about it is far less effective.*

Without the opportunity to practise a skill or technique an effective
transfer to the workplace does not happen.

In the example described above, the consultants involved had
never run a workshop before and implicitly believed a formal lecture-
based approach would give them more control of events. They were
pleasantly surprised by the enjoyment they and the participants
gained from a more interactive approach.

So what do you need to do to make workshops effective?

Set your objectives

What is the purpose of the workshop? What is the end result that you
need to achieve?

Determine an appropriate structure

For someone new to training this apparently simple task can be a
minefield. The following steps will help you:

- brainstorm the issues you need to cover during the workshop.
- break these into chunks that appear manageable and allocate time accordingly.
- now revisit your timing and ask yourself – can we achieve real learning in the time available? Most of us seriously underestimate the time it actually takes for someone to absorb information, question it, practise and get feedback.
- think about the 'how' of the workshop – how can learning be made enjoyable and effective? So consider the mix between lectures, role plays, practical tasks and case studies. Table 5.1 shows some pros and cons.

Fig. 5.2 shows an example of a workshop structure which shows the overall approach and themes. It shows how 'chunks' have been identified and sessions planned accordingly.

Having established the overall structure, you should break each session into detailed tasks and develop a short guide to ensure you cover the appropriate ground as shown in Fig. 5.3. Without such a guide it is very easy for an inexperienced workshop leader to ignore key areas or find time runs out.

Feedback

How will participants get feedback on their progress? What action will need to be taken after the workshop to ensure understanding has been translated into action? In this context the coaching skills referred to earlier will play a key role. Merely asking for feedback at the end of the day is not sufficient. All you will get is an instant answer. So consider checking back a week or a month later to see if the knowledge/skills imparted have been retained and are being utilised. If not, explore the cause and consider whether the workshop format needs altering.

MANAGING PROGRESS MEETINGS

Most of us have experience of attending meetings which failed to achieve their intended purpose. For the internal consultant they are

	What is it/How it works	Advantages	Disadvantages
Case Study	A situation for discussion on – e.g. (a) determining causes of problem (b) solving a problem	Provides opportunities for exchange of ideas and consideration of possible solutions. Useful in shaping attitudes. Proposed solutions can be compared with actual action taken.	Wrong impression may be conveyed by written brief. Time consuming. Participants may not transfer experience from case study to reality of their current work environment.
Brainstorming	Thoughts on problem brought out in quick-fire succession. Discussion of solutions does not take place until after brainstorming.	Quick method of making people feel involved. Ideas freely expressed as they are bounced off one another. Works well with large groups. Forms a sound basis for group discussion.	Can be slow to start and therefore needs good introduction. Must have flipcharts available and quick writers to write down comments.
Lecture	Can be entirely one-way or can allow participation through questions or discussions.	Quick way of putting over information to groups where speaker has monopoly of information	No way of assessing what has been learned without building in feedback.
Role Play	Participants are allocated roles in a situation which enables subsequent review of behaviour – e.g. conducting a disciplinary interview.	Practical, well written role plays can produce lively and useful learning.	Some participants may find them 'phoney'. Feedback on performance must be handled carefully.

Table 5.1 Pros and cons of various workshop techniques

TRAIN THE TRAINER

Day One

SESSION ONE –	Course introduction	9.00 – 9.30
	Objectives of course	
SESSION TWO –	Why Train?	9.30–10.30
SESSION THREE –	How people learn?	10.45–12.00
	Who are we training?	12.00 – 1.00
SESSION FOUR –	Setting objectives and	2.00 – 3.30
	evaluating training	
	Preparation of talk/discussion	3.45 – 4.30

Day Two

SESSION FIVE –	Giving feedback	9.00–10.15
	Visual aids	10.30–11.20
SESSION SIX –	Discussion – talk	11.20–3.30 (inc. lunch)
	Handling questions	3.45 – 5.00

Day Three

SESSION SEVEN –	Methods of training	9.00–10.30
SESSION EIGHT –	Job instruction	10.45–3.45 (inc. lunch)
	Course close	4.00

Fig. 5.2 Sample workshop structure

SESSION ONE: INTRODUCTION   9.00 – 9.30

Purpose: To outline the purpose, objectives and format of the course, and to share participants learning goals.

Timing: *Notes*

9.00   Welcome participants
                   Course introductions   [use overhead slide]

                   Participants introductions

                   - name
                   - background
                   - involvement in training

                   Describe format of the course:

                   - participative, designed to stimulate
                     discussion and action,

                   - no 'right' answers – we will discuss approaches,
                     share ideas and agree some best points of practice,

                   - eight sessions over three days,

                   - mixture of individual work, teamwork
                     and group work,

                   - presentations, exercises and discussion.

                   Cover 'ground rules' for the course:

                   - be on time,
                   - participate actively,
                   - listen generously,
                   - help others to learn,
                   - help others to teach.

Fig. 5.3 Sample workshop timetable

both a shop window in which to demonstrate progress so far but also an opportunity to tap into emergent themes, test out new ideas, and identify potential problem areas ahead. Once again the 'basics' are important determinants of success: the structure of the meeting, as evidenced by the agenda, how the meeting is run, and what happens as a consequence. Before reviewing these it is worth exploring the context within which meetings will take place during a project. There will be regularly scheduled progress meetings, but there may also be 'one off' meetings of individuals, perhaps with specific expertise. Less likely, but sometimes necessary, will be 'crisis' meetings if a project is running badly behind schedule, or if significant unanticipated problems have occurred.

As an internal consultant you may be very familiar with the way meetings run, but in a large organisation different divisions or departments may have significantly different approaches. External consultants are frequently surprised by the chaotic approach to meetings in ostensibly well-managed businesses. In these situations the most common refrain is 'don't worry we take our clients much more seriously than we do ourselves!' Thus meetings starting late, over-running by some hours, with people popping in and out are seen as the norm.

In other situations the tone may be set by the approach adopted by the senior executive. These may be characterised by faultless timing, but virtually no debate on issues, with the view – or prejudice – of the Chairman determining action.

For the smooth running of your project, and it might be said for your peace of mind, it will be helpful to ensure that participants to meetings in which you are involved either as chairman or main presenter agree to stick by some behaviourial ground rules. These should cover:

- timekeeping: everyone will be busy on other projects etc. so agree that you will all help each other by being punctual.
- attendance: as far as possible those nominated to attend should do so. In other words only in extremes should a deputy be sent. There is one principal reason for this. At a typical project progress meeting discussions will take place on the next phase of work.

Unless all participants have a clear grasp of the overall approach being adopted you will not get a fully representative picture and neither will other participants. The progress meeting may be the only occasion when the senior line managers responsible for the project get together and hence share in a collective view of the project and its progress.

In the event that a 'crisis' meeting needs to be convened this collective dimension may become especially important, since if the scope of the project needs to be changed or the schedule amended, the buy-in of all key players is essential.

Example: An organisation was about to embark on a major change programme following an investigative programme by a team of consultants. Two weeks before this ambitious programme was to begin there was a significant shift in the external market. The consultants proposed a meeting of the Operations Committee (a sub-committee of the Board) to review the situation and ensure the senior team, whose commitment was so vital, were prepared for the project to go ahead. The meeting was convened and after lengthy discussion and debate the Operations Committee re-asserted their commitment. Afterwards a key question for the consultants was 'would the Operations Committee have met without their instigation?'

What aspects do you need to manage if your meetings are to be successful?

Composition

However complex the project, a progress meeting of more than twelve participants is unlikely to be successful. Indeed the optimum number is between five and seven.

The Agenda

The agenda serves to:

● provide information about the purpose of the meeting;

- identify the content of the meeting;
- provide a means to identify the length of time required;
- ensure the appropriate people attend.

Without an agenda progress meetings are prone to be railroaded by topics which may be 'nice' to discuss rather than 'need' to be reviewed. The consultant needs to be clear that the progress meeting is an integral part of the project management process. As such you need to be clear about what may – and may not – be accomplished. The agenda for a progress meeting must include:

- results to date;
- budget situation;
- any problems encountered;
- decisions required;
- what will be accomplished between now and the next meeting.

You should ensure that you are responsible for the production of the agenda. You will probably find few others willing to do what is often seen as a chore but in the event that someone else does prepare the agenda, you must ensure that you see it before it goes out, and if necessary ask for changes to be made.

Running the meeting

A structured agenda must be accompanied by active chairmanship of the meeting. Who chairs the meeting depends on the circumstances. In some cases a complex project may well be overseen by a steering group of client personnel and consultants with the most senior client manager 'in the chair'. In such cases the internal consultant will need to have a pre-meeting, with the chairperson to plan the meeting. In other cases your client may be very happy for you to chair the meetings.

Whether you are chairing the meeting or not you have a key role to play in ensuring things run to plan. This includes:

- **structuring discussion.** From time to time meetings get sidetracked – perhaps two or three participants reflect on a problem they are handling at the present time, or digress into reviewing operating problems in a particular department. You need to ensure that the meeting sticks to relevant issues.

- **managing the time.** This follows from the structure of the meeting. A poorly structured meeting will waste time and irritate participants.
- **observe participants.** You must listen to contributions and observe the participants. Is everyone contributing? Is there open or covert disagreement on key issues. You can assist the process of mutual understanding by:
  - rephrasing and repetition, to clarify what is actually meant;
  - asking questions to explore **why** a particular view is held;
  - getting everyone's view on a subject to get latent disagreement into the open.
- **airtime.** Whatever the meeting all participants will unconsciously have a notion of 'airtime'. In other words the time during the meeting when they get to 'contribute'. We can become so concerned about the need to make a personal contribution to a meeting that we focus not on the ebb and flow of discussion but upon spotting and seizing a window of opportunity in which to speak. It follows that if all participants are doing this at the same time, little real discussion takes place.
- **ground rules.** Taking all the above points into account it would seem commonsense to agree with participants at the first meeting what the ground rules for discussion will be. Unfortunately commonsense is not always common practice. The risk is that if you are seen to be overly dominant at the first meeting it may inhibit participants saying what they really feel. The best bet is to see how the first discussion progresses and ask for ten minutes at the end to review with everyone how effective they feel the meeting was. At this point you can coach participants in a constructive manner.

After the meeting

What happens after the progress meeting? Hopefully actions are agreed and responsibilities allocated during the meeting. But, to get things to happen it is important that action points are confirmed in writing and as quickly as possible after the meeting. To get this to happen you should volunteer to produce these notes.

PRESENTING RESULTS AND DELIVERING REPORTS THAT HAVE IMPACT

The view that consultants are only as good as their last job may be something of a cliché. However, whether you like it or not, as an internal consultant, it is also in large measure absolutely correct. And how will your client assess the impact your project has had? Whilst in the medium and longer term it will be through measurable/assessable results in the immediate aftermath of the project it will be upon how your results are presented.

Keep checking with your client on what they expect

Your terms of reference and proposal document will have indicated the results and benefits to be achieved by your project. But they may not have been absolutely specific. So first and foremost you must agree with your client at the outset of the project the date by which your results will be presented, to whom, and in what format. This may appear to be stating the obvious, but it raises important issues for the internal consultant. Thus you may be operating in a culture where written reports are very much the norm. Your judgement may incline you towards presenting the results via workshops supported by summaries of key data and findings. Be warned: your client may see this as risky or even an attempt by you to avoid giving value for money. If you are sure you are right you must be able to show your client an example of the approach you propose using.

Some key considerations are:

- get your timing right – if you promise the report by a particular date deliver it – your client will not easily forgive poor presentation caused by software problems or an 'incompetent temp'.
- if you are presenting your findings at a meeting do you need to talk your client/sponsor through a draft to gain comment/acceptance of

your perspective? Few of us like surprises and your client will be no exception.

- give particular thought to the shape of the presentation/report in the light of the audience that will review it. Remind the reader of terms of reference, people interviewed and identify commitments impacting on delivery. This needs especial attention if you are a lone internal consultant. For whilst the extensive checks and balances employed by large consultancies may ensure that a draft goes through a number of alterations there is a real risk that you won't have someone to double-check your logic before present-ation to the client.
- an issue for the internal consultant is who is going to prepare your results. It would not be surprising if someone reading this book were about to embark on a sensitive project involving:
  - restructuring
  - downsizing
  - senior management competencies
- So who will prepare your report/slides? Swearing the MD's secre-tary to silence when they are being asked to type a damning review of their boss's last initiative may not be enough.

Delivering written reports that have impact

It is worth reminding ourselves of the rule of thirds. Consulting is

- one third fact finding
- one third analysis and development of recommendations
- one third report writing

For your client the visible tip of a rather large iceberg representing substantial toil and effort will be your report. It must make the correct impression. Contrast the impact of 'poor' and 'effective' reports:

Poor reports

Most poor reports suffer from a failure to recognise that their prime purpose is to communicate.

The language is often verbose and uses unnecessary jargon. The layout – long sentences, long paragraphs, lack of headings and sub-headings – often hinders the reader's understanding. There is no clear structure, so the reader has difficulty following the argument and identifying the main points. Important facts are missing, and others are wrong. There is often confusion between verifiable facts and the writer's opinion. Finally a bad report is often over-long because of failure to identify its precise purpose, including exactly what its readers need to get from it.

Effective reports

Effective reports, avoiding the above failings, are created by following the Rule of the Four Cs. The report should be:

CLEAR   CONCISE   COMPLETE   CORRECT

- A *clear* report is one that the reader will be able to understand at first reading.
- A *concise* report is one in which the information is kept down to an intelligent and intelligible minimum. It is as long as it needs to be, but no longer.
- A *complete* report is one in which all the necessary information is included, with nothing truly relevant left out.
- A *correct* report is one in which every piece of information is accurate and verifiable; and with opinion and interpretation always identified.

Impact

Advances in desk top publishing have dramatically enhanced the impact of reports. But there has been another change. Once upon a time a client may have expected a multi-volume report to demonstrate the significance of your work. This is no longer the case, particularly in the context of internal consulting. Recession and competition have enhanced the importance of a 'real time' approach to presenting reports. The use of hard copies of overhead slides which carry key information is increasingly the norm but the basics of good report writing still apply. The following examples show the distinction between 'poor' and 'effective' presentation quite dramatically. Consider the impact the first, muddled, presentation can have (Fig. 5.4): it confuses, and raises more questions than answers. The second example (Fig. 5.5) uses information more sparingly and allows the reader to focus on what is relevant.

Notwithstanding this there will of course be many occasions when more substantial data needs to be presented – e.g. feasibility studies or attitude surveys. Think about the last report you had to read – did it leave a lasting impression? If not, why not? Frequently a report can 'lose' the reader through poor structure, inadequate discussion of key arguments, and insufficient emphasis on what the implications of the report are. Table 5.2 looks at the 'typical' content of an effective report and the rationale of the content.

One approach which may help in determining what goes where in the report is to go through the following sequence.

- use brainstorming to generate as many ideas as possible on the themes the report needs to cover.
- cluster these into major streams.
- develop an overall structure for the report.
- for each chapter develop a draft structure and cluster information into major streams.

You don't have to write the report in the order in which it is to be read. As you write, keep in mind the readers and remind yourself that **they**, not you, must understand your words. Read the draft and be critical:

- are the facts correct?
- is anything missing? Can anything be omitted?
- is the report relevant?
- do conclusions and recommendations flow logically from the facts/findings?
- does it read easily?
- build in a deadline plan.

For the inexperienced consultant producing a detailed project report can be difficult. The pure task of pulling information together

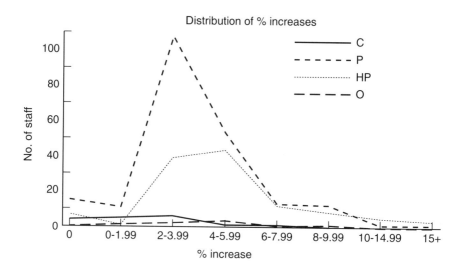

Fig. 5.4 Example of poor presentation of data

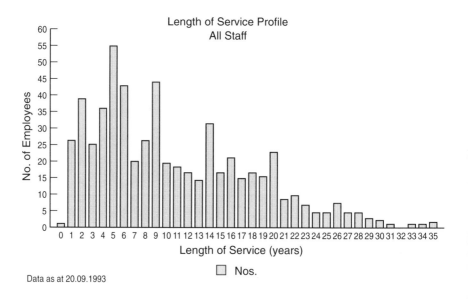

Fig. 5.5 Example of clear presentation of data

Table 5.2 Typical content of an effective report

Section	Comment
INTRODUCTION	All reports need this!
Executive Summary	This is a one- or two-page summary of key issues and findings.
Background	What lies behind this report – is it in response to a company-wide initiative? Has it been promoted by a change in legislation?
Purpose of report	This is the link with your terms of reference.
APPROACH	How you went about your work: organisations/departments visited; use of interviews; methodologies used.
Structure of report	This is the section which tells the reader what is coming next.
Acknowledgements	It is usual to thank people who have helped you.
Successive chapters should have their own brief introduction and focus in a structured manner on the key aspects of the project. These are facts/findings and should not be confused with recommendations.	
Conclusions and recommendations	Here you should review what you have presented and look forward to what next?
Cost and benefits	Your readers will need to understand the implications of any recommendations you are making.
Appendices	You should not clutter up your text with masses of detail. Appendices can cover such things as those people interviewed; the detail of a cash-flow analysis model; data upon which key findings are based.

and creating an appropriate structure takes far longer than most consultants anticipate. Equally the logistics of report production need to be sensibly managed – who will do your typing? How many copies are required? Who will check and recheck the finished work?

One technique which large consultancies practise is to provide a 'discussion draft' of their report. This is precisely what the name implies, a draft for discussion with the client. Such a document enables you to check on client understanding and satisfaction before a final copy is prepared. Moreover it avoids the risk of surprising the client.

INFLUENCING TACTICS 'AS PRACTISED BY PROFESSIONAL CONSULTANTS'

For the internal consultant it is crucial to create a climate around a project which enhances the likelihood that recommendations will be accepted. This can be a particular challenge when the internal consultant is perceived as junior or inexperienced in traditional hierarchical terms. However, this is a challenge which all consultants have to confront a number of times during their professional careers. Thus:

- how do you establish credibility during your first project when the organisation is aware that this is the case?
- how do you deal with Board members when you have not experienced Board-level management yourself?

In part the answer is to do with positioning yourself as the expert and being fairly sanguine about what projects are within your ability to complete competently. Furthermore think about what you may be influencing your clients to do. It could be:

- to gain acceptance of your recommendations;
- to get the client to put forward their own point of view;
- to get the client to **take responsibility** for the project's recommendations;
- to actually implement the recommendations.

What should your general approach be?

It is impossible to be didactic as you need to adopt a style which suits you and is appropriate to the situation. Most of us will certainly have experienced different approaches. The continuum is wide as the following descriptions show:

- some consultants are quietly persuasive and would see themselves as guiding their clients on the basis of high-quality research and recommendations.
- others would see themselves as having to be fairly assertive with their client if the project is to be delivered on time and on budget. This is the 'this just won't do' approach where the client is made very aware as to what is required of them. This approach may not be to everyone's taste, but there are undeniably circumstances where it may be vital that your client is left in absolutely no doubt as to your concerns. A downsizing or cost-containment project, for example, might call for this.
- in projects involving high-level business strategy a relationship may develop which is much more balanced, with mutual support and challenge very much in evidence.

The key word is **appropriate.** Thus you may have a client who is uncertain, unwilling, or unco-operative and each will have different needs. So review yourself against the descriptions below which distinguish assertive, non-assertive, and aggressive behaviour.

How assertive are you?

Assertiveness is an essential skill in dealing with people. It may be defined as: stating needs, wants, opinions, feelings and beliefs in direct, honest and appropriate ways. It is an important skill because it is more likely to:

- lead to a productive exchange and beneficial outcome;
- leave you and the other person feeling at ease, which means that;
- future exchanges with that person are also more likely to be productive.

Assertive behaviour is best understood by contrasting it with less effective non-assertive and aggressive styles.

Assertive behaviour involves:

- standing up for your own position but not at the expense of other people – i.e. having respect for the position of others, understanding their point of view, being prepared to negotiate and having the confidence to do so, but not entirely at your own expense. It is a way of effectively handling potentially difficult situations to mutual benefit.

Non-assertive behaviour involves:

- failing to state your needs, wants, opinions, feelings and beliefs, or stating them in a way that makes it easy for others to disregard them – e.g. being apologetic.

Non-assertiveness often means putting up with a situation which makes you feel angry internally, rather than being honest about what you really think or feel – e.g. failing to draw attention to poor quality service in a restaurant.

Aggressive behaviour involves:

- ignoring or dismissing the needs, wants, opinions, feelings or beliefs of others, or expressing your own needs in inappropriate ways.

Being aggressive means getting your own way at the expense of other people, for example by putting them down, or manipulating them.

What to do

Throughout a project there will be numerous occasions when you need to exert influence with your client. They may be concerned that progress is not being made; may have concerns about the methodology you are using; or may even have got cold feet, having failed to anticipate the impact the project would have. So you may have to use influence to respond to criticism, to regain the initiative, or to gain commitment.

Getting co-operation

More generally there will always be occasions when a key individual is unco-operative. In these circumstances your relationships with the client are key, as is their commitment to the exercise. Professional consultants will always attempt to keep the initiative during a project. They will continually assess progress, notably against the terms of reference but also in a more qualitative sense:

- how are things going?
- where are the pressure points? Why?
- are we getting the support/commitment that was promised? If not, why not?

However, don't confuse being liked with being respected. Rather than saying things to please in the heat of the moment it is much more effective to do your homework before meetings and to lobby before them to gain support for your point of view.

Responding to criticism

Should your client make critical remarks about your project, two key attributes will stand you in good stead: keeping your emotions under control and providing rational answers. These are explored in more depth below.

- keeping your emotions under control involves the following steps:
  - listen;
  - pause and think;
  - acknowledge their concern;
  - allow them to own their 'feelings'
  - get the specific concern into the open.
- provide rational answers
  - for example by turning the concern into a question;
  - establish the need behind the concern;
  - be honest.

It is worth examining one key aspect of this process in more detail, that of listening skills. Most managers – and consultants are no exception – are not good listeners. Perhaps this has something to do with a natural desire 'to get the job done' or an indifference to the impact we are making on the speaker. And whilst we may **think** we are listening we may appear as preoccupied or distracted. Picture the following exchange of views between a client and their consultant:

Client: *'I've got some real concerns that some of your team just don't seem to understand our business. It's as if they're going to meetings with a pre-packaged solution'.*

Consultant: *'Well, we're using a hand-picked team here . . .'*

                At the same time the consultant will be thinking: 'what's gone wrong' . . . 'I bet it was so and so'.

   The reality may be that the client has been presented with a partial picture by colleagues who for one reason or another wish to deflect a particular proposition. Of course it could be absolutely accurate comment. The difficulty is that the consultant's first comment is creating a barrier. What should an effective consultant do?

Keep an open mind

When the speaker says something with which the listener strongly disagrees, the listener should continue to listen attentively and search their own mind for evidence which might support the speaker's point of view. On the other hand, if the speaker says something with which the listener agrees instinctively, they should search their mind for evidence that might prove them both wrong.

Think ahead of the speaker

We think much more quickly than we speak and it is often possible to think ahead of the speaker and predict what they are going to say. The good listener does this and then, rather than 'switching off' on the assumption that their prediction is correct, listens carefully to see what the speaker actually says. In this way, whether the speaker says what was expected or something unexpected, the listener is more likely to remember what was said.

Summarise what has been said

Whether or not the speaker summarises what they have said, the good listener should note down the main points the speaker makes and review them whenever they have an opportunity. In this way they not only increase their chances of understanding and remembering what has been said, but also create a sound basis for subsequent discussion.

Listen between the lines

The good listener not only listens to what is being said but also tries to penetrate behind the words to the speaker's thoughts and state of mind. How a speaker says something is often more important than what they say. Listening between the lines can be done successfully only if the listener is able to control their emotions, suspend their judgement and search for the truth with a truly open mind.

Remember that your client will above all want **reassurance**. They will want to know that you the project manager have the situation under control. Your client's reaction may be a mixture of emotional and rational concerns.

Regaining the initiative and gaining commitment

These two very frequently go hand in hand. Maybe initial enthusiasm for the project is fading, a not surprising result given the demands on people in organisations these days. The influencing tactics you can deploy cover a wide spectrum ranging from a direct request for commitment to concessions which may result in conducting certain aspects of the project in a different manner **but** without compromising the end result.

Direct request

Example: 'Without an increased level of commitment from line managers we won't be able to bring the project in on schedule. If certain key managers do not attend the workshops we are running on the new job evaluation scheme they will be unable to explain it to their own teams and play into the trade unions' objections that the proposed new scheme is unworkable'.

In this instance the direct request did the trick. The Chief Executive held a special briefing session to re-energise his 'lieutenants'.

Commend

Example: 'Based on our experience if you don't confront the concerns employees have now their fears will multiply. You could of course wait a bit longer but we feel it's important that you arrange to speak to the Staff Liaison Committee.'

Again this worked.

Concede

If there **is** another way of doing something, think about it. Hence a request that you 'reposition the start of the second stage of the project to reflect a change in the order processing arrangements in the distribution centre' may leave you with no choice.

Self-awareness

Take a look at your own behaviour in the light of experience and beware of the following:

● coming across as a waffler. Most of us need thinking time. Some consultants, however, appear to take rather a long time to think and can fill this time with a meaningless commentary that weakens their position. Be honest; if you need some time to think about a question, say so.

- don't on any account promise what you cannot deliver. This aspect raises a number of concerns for the internal consultant eager to create a demand for their services. We have seen that poor work planning can catch you out, so never give an 'off the cuff' response. Clarify with the client exactly what is required. There is also the issue of integrity and ensuring that you do not place yourself in a situation of conflict of interest. For example your client suggests that as well as reviewing the IT strategy the business will require over the next three to five years you will 'no doubt be able to comment on the calibre of the staff'. Your response is along the lines: 'I'm sure we'll be able to provide some insights into opportunities for staff development'. This is construed by the client as meaning you will be able to give a yes/no view of the continued employment of the IT Director.

- managing expectations. Two magic words all consultants would do well to remember are 'no surprises'. Throughout the project ensure that you are in a position to provide a snapshot on progress and if anything starts to occur which could create difficulties sensitise your client to it. This is not to be confused with **ALARM**. In other words: 'as we noted in our proposal, getting hold of some of your underwriters was always going to be tricky in November and December. So far we've seen a couple but it may be that three key people won't be available. If this does prove to be the case we'll need to jointly think about the impact on our progress'.

COST AND BENEFIT ANALYSIS OF RECOMMENDATIONS

What are the costs and benefits of your recommendations? Are the costs so great as to make a proposed course of action untenable? Can the benefits be quantified or are they very much an act of faith? A cost and benefit analysis is one way of proving your worth to the client. This may be particularly appropriate when the benefits considerably outweigh the costs.

What will it take to implement your recommendations?

Two distinct and differing client views:

- 'as you know, the changes you are proposing are very much an act of faith, . . . but let's just have a look at the figures first'.
- 'if this change programme is as significant as you (the consultants) suggest, we shouldn't make our minds up on the basis of the numbers . . . if we get this right we will accrue much more significant benefits than the figures suggest in the form of new approaches to working and innovation.'

The impact of, and reaction to, your recommendations will depend heavily upon the organisational context and the needs of your client. A cost containment programme as opposed to an investment in total quality management would be likely to generate different priorities in terms of costs and benefits. However, whatever the circumstances, your client will be concerned with the relationship between the following:

- the cost of taking action;
- the risk of acting or doing nothing;
- the benefits to be gained;
- the certainty that action will lead to gain, and,
- the time frame within which the cost-benefit relationship will be measured.

There are a number of ways to review these relationships. In straightforward cost terms will the one-off benefit of a recommendation be greater or less than the one-off cost of implementation? In reality, other factors to take into account will include the 'hassle' factor associated with making things happen and any long-term repetitive benefit which may accrue.

The optimum use of capital necessitates the need to evaluate projects with a common standard of financial return or benefit. Techniques such as assessment of payback period, the return on investment and discounted cash flow can all be used to assist the process of quantifying benefits. However, most projects are unlikely to be based solely on the delivery of 'hard' quantitative benefits.

More likely are recommendations which will deliver qualitative benefits which can be expected to produce quantitative benefits over time. Of importance here is the need for benefits tracking – i.e. what by when, and an initial assessment of the range of benefits which may be capable of delivery.

Opportunity cost

One key aspect in balancing up the pros and cons of a particular course of action will be the opportunity cost. Whilst the anticipated initial cost of a recommendation may be conservative in terms of consultant effort required, there may be substantial internal costs. If managers are deployed to assist in developing, say, a new marketing strategy, what will this activity prevent them doing?

A number of studies of the implementation of major projects have consistently emphasised cost/benefit issues such as:

- implementation taking more time than originally expected;
- problems occurring during implementation that had not been expected;
- problems created by poor co-ordination mechanisms;
- other problems – or crises – emerging during the project implementation which distract attention.

Consequently you should not be surprised to be challenged. Many of your clients will ruefully reflect on 'promised' benefits from other projects which never fully materialised. The matrix in Fig. 5.6 shows an approach to distinguishing between the type of benefits available.

An example of this approach is shown in Fig. 5.7.

It allows consultant and client to focus on both 'hard' and 'soft' issues and to explore whether non-quantified, non-financial benefits can actually be realised.

The example (Fig. 5.8) shows the anticipated benefits and costs from a multi-functional management development programme. Here the issues will be: can the first order benefits actually be attained and what can – and should – we do to minimise the 'cost' implications?

The approach in Fig. 5.8 takes into account benefits and costs.

	Finanical	**Non-financial**
Quantified	An improvement where financial impact is clearly identified and measurable	An improvement which has a non-financial but measurable impact
Non-quantified	An improvement which has a financial impact that cannot be accurately estimated	An improvement which represents noticeable and real progress but in a way that cannot be measured accurately

Fig. 5.6 Generic benefits matrix

	Finanical	**Non-financial**
Quantified	e.g. improved cash management = increased investment income	e.g. improved internal liaison = fewer, shorter meetings
Non-quantified	e.g. potential revenues from enhanced client management skills = customer development	e.g. improved order processing = increased employee morale = improved customer relationship

Fig. 5.7 Sample benefits matrix

Inevitably this approach, showing opportunities, will require clarification. Clients will frequently argue that even if the proposed approach were not to be adopted, 'other' initiatives would no doubt be implemented which could produce similar benefit. The issue here may very much reside in the confidence your client has in the approp-

First order benefits	Second order benefits
• Broadens the individual • Allows 'blue sky' thinking • Creates and sustains wider networking	• Helps to develop general management talent • Enhances adaptiveness and innovation
First order costs	**Second order costs**
• Could place individuals in jobs for which they lack necessary technical expertise • Possible resentment amongst subordinates	• Dilutes functional strengths • May create pressure on salaries • Could de-motivate certain functional specialists

Fig. 5.8 Sample costs/benefits matrix

riateness of a particular course of action. As an internal consultant you should be well placed to assess the cost/risk of doing nothing from an in-house perspective. What your analysis will also need to consider are developments elsewhere, for example what are the competition up to? How might the market change? What is the likely cost of doing nothing?

6

HOW TO MEASURE SUCCESS

This is a particularly important area for the internal consultant. A key issue is ongoing quality assurance throughout consulting projects and beyond. This requires effective engagement management, and the use of customer satisfaction surveys and other techniques. These can be used to measure client satisfaction; the extent to which recommendations are being implemented effectively; and whether they are bringing the desired benefits to the organisation.

What does quality mean in the context of internal consulting? Three things, in particular:

- adhering to standards of professional practice, in terms of the application of technical knowledge, principles of effective consulting and standards of ethics and conduct.
- effective project administration, involving among other things the maintenance of project files and records systems. This is important to facilitate your own work and also the smooth transition of responsibility from consultant to client. BS5750 can be of value towards achieving efficiency and high standards.
- above all, giving clients sound advice that meets their needs and those of the organisation. This is the most difficult as well as the most important aspect of quality, requiring the most rigorous monitoring.

Falling down on your quality standards will cause problems both for your clients and for you. Ultimately, if you fail to deliver what your clients need in a timely and efficient manner you will fail to win further work. You must, therefore, measure quality and the extent to which your projects achieve their objectives and contribute to the clients success.

MONITORING PROJECT PROGRESS AND CLIENT SATISFACTION

You should never assume that a client is satisfied just because they don't pass adverse comment on work you are doing for them. A well-known statistic established by market research is that, for every dissatisfied customer who complains about service quality there are likely to be as many as ten who say nothing. This can be just as true in consulting as anywhere else. There is, therefore, a strong onus on the consultant to monitor levels of quality and client satisfaction, both during a project and after it has come to an end.

Quality monitoring during a project

As a professional consultant, you should be committed to delivering quality work to your clients at all times. This means you need regularly to monitor your quality standards during project work, either on your own or with assistance from colleagues.

Delivering high-quality consulting work to clients involves:

- developing an understanding of the clients needs and agreeing these with the client. Check: were these needs properly explored in drawing up the terms of reference, and is there evidence to prove this? Are the needs addressed directly by the deliverables of the project?
- designing a project framework that enables you to address the clients needs. Check: are the project phases proving to be realistic in terms of the work content, timescales and resources specified? Are other consultants or counterparts selected for the project proving up to their tasks?
- throughout the work programme, adhering to the project framework so that the work progresses smoothly, in a logical sequence and within the required timescale. Check: is there a

smooth transition from one project phase to the next, or is it necessary to recap or carry out additional work before progress into successive phases can be made?

- maintaining contact with the client throughout the project so that he/she is aware of progress, any required amendments to the work programme are agreed and there are no 'nasty surprises'. Check: have regular meetings taken place, and been documented? Is the client being kept abreast of progress? Is the client remaining involved in the work, for example through participation in workshops/presentations, counterpart involvement in fact-finding and analysis?

- ensuring that research and other routine tasks are carried out thoroughly and accurately, and are recorded fully for future reference. Check: are you keeping notes of fact-finding meetings? Have any areas of fact-finding been skimped or omitted?

- ensuring that recommendations made are supported by research and can be explained/justified to the client. Check: have recommendations been documented, is the thinking behind them logical, taking account of the results of research? Have they been discussed with the client? Has the clients response to recommendations been documented fully?

- producing written reports and presentations that are clear and well prepared. Check: have reports/presentations been understood by the client? Have any issues emerged that were not included?

- ensuring the project deliverables address the clients needs and meet his/her expectations. Check: are they as specified in the terms of reference? Have they been delivered on time? Do they take account of any modifications to the project emerging from dialogue with the client that has taken place throughout the project?

Monitoring these quality areas requires a certain self-discipline, above all the ability to question yourself and the progress you are making measured against the original terms of reference of the project. You should develop the habit of reviewing your quality standards informally on a fortnightly, if not weekly basis. More formally, you should carry out a more thorough review at the end of each project phase.

For small projects or where you are a sole practitioner, you may have to carry out this review by yourself. For larger projects, it can be done in conjunction with peers (i.e. other consultants working in your practice) or the project manager who is in overall control of the work you do. You should not regard the involvement of other parties in the review process as a threat; on the contrary, it can be extremely valuable to have the input of people who are not directly involved in the work, and can address issues and problems on a more independent basis.

Project quality reviews

It is common practice amongst the major external consulting firms for project quality reviews to take place, in which either every project is reviewed on completion or a sample of completed projects is subjected to a thorough quality analysis at periodic intervals. The objective is to determine the extent to which projects conform to professional practice, as defined by the consulting firm: not so much to criticise or comment on the conduct of the consultants concerned, as to monitor overall client service quality standards.

Reviews are usually carried out by senior consultants or managers who have had no involvement in the project itself, to ensure independence. If you are in a small internal consulting practice, it can be difficult to find anyone appropriate to carry out such reviews. There may be no other consultants with the necessary degree of independence, and it is unlikely anyone else in the organisation will have sufficient understanding of your profession to be suitable. However, where the practice is large or diverse enough to enable project quality reviews, the opportunity to implement them should not be dismissed. They are an excellent means of both framing and monitoring the professional standards of an internal consultancy.

Project quality reviews should include all the areas covered during ongoing project quality monitoring, although because they are less immediate they focus much more strongly on documentation such as the terms of reference/workplan, interim and final reports, meeting notes and project files. Evidence of high professional standards looked for might therefore include:

- a thorough and detailed workplan including timescales and budgets;
- regular documentation of actual time spent by each consultant involved during the project;
- full documentation of research carried out;
- the extent to which consideration has been given to different solutions before reaching definite conclusions;
- the extent to which implementation plans for recommendations have been drawn up and documented;
- evidence of regular communication with the client, such as progress meetings;
- evidence of regular communication between the members of the project team where more than one consultant is involved;
- reports and presentation material delivered to the client on time and to high standards of completeness and clarity;
- properly maintained project files;
- adherence to procedures in charging clients for work done;
- any evidence of client satisfaction with the work programme.

On completion of a project quality review, a report setting out the main findings should be prepared and issued to all consultants involved in the project. This should be balanced, highlighting good points as well as any where improvements are recommended. Remember, the purpose of the review is to improve professional practice overall rather than knock the work of individual consultants.

Client satisfaction surveys and interviews

However rigorously it is carried out, project quality monitoring by consultants themselves can only go part of the way towards establishing quality standards and finding out what clients really think about the service they receive. It is essential, therefore, to approach clients directly to find out their views.

These approaches should take place shortly, though not necessary immediately, after completion of the project. In most cases a delay of between one and four weeks following completion is best, enabling the impact of the project to be felt and a more measured response to be given. In an ideal world, it would be possible to conduct structured interviews with all clients to obtain as much information as possible. Where there are a large number of clients this may not be possible, however, and it may be necessary to select a sample of clients to be interviewed. Alternatively, issuing a questionnaire to clients may be considered sufficient. It should be borne in mind however that it is better to obtain detailed information from a selection of your clients than sketchy information from all your clients. When responding to sensitive questions people have a tendency to gloss over the truth and this can lead to a falsely positive view of service standards emerging. If you want to find out the true picture, far better to spend some time in face-to-face interviews with a few key clients, and get their in-depth views on how the project succeeded.

Who should you interview? Certainly your main client contact, and ideally the project sponsor as well if this is a different person. If you are selecting a sample of clients, you should aim to include some for whom you have carried out larger, more complex projects, and those who you see as possibilities for further work. You should also include any clients where you know or suspect there have been problems in carrying out the project: there is no point in just ignoring their views, you need to know about your failures if you are to improve your performance in the future.

Your interviews should be based on a properly designed questionnaire, and you should use the same questionnaire in interviewing all selected clients. The areas you should cover in the questionnaire are:

- professional skills: what did the client think of your understanding of the organisation/business, and his/her role within it? Did you demonstrate understanding of the client's main issues and needs? Did you have a sound knowledge of technical issues? Was research carried out thoroughly and accurately? Did you show good analytical skills in problem-solving and solution development? Are your recommendations proving to be workable following implementation?
- client relations: did you meet the project deadlines, were you

available to the client when needed and did you respond promptly to questions? Did you establish good working relationships with client counterparts and other staff involved in the project? Were you proactive in reporting on progress? Were your written reports and presentations clear, relevant and informative?

- benefits gained: did the project meet its objectives in full – if not, in what areas did it fall short? Were your recommendations and solutions practical? Above all, what benefits have resulted from implementation of your recommendations?

- overall satisfaction with your work: how satisfied was the client with your services in each of the areas where you gave consulting support? Would the client be willing to use your services again, or recommend you to other managers?

If you cover all this ground during your interviews you should emerge with a very good indication of whether or not your project was a success. You should aim to draw out as much qualitative information as possible from interviewees, and should take notes of all comments or suggestions made. Following each interview you should review these notes and establish whether there are any immediate action points to be taken. There may be any number of easily rectified, relatively minor problems relating to project management or professional conduct that impact on the success of your projects.

When you have carried out a number of client satisfaction interviews, a broad picture should emerge of your strengths and weaknesses. This may lead you into a more fundamental review of aspects of your consulting practice. It can be valuable to inform your clients of the results of your research and any actions you have taken in consequence. This demonstrates to them your commitment to quality improvement, and that you take notice of their views.

In summary, carrying out client satisfaction surveys is a key aspect of professional internal consulting, which can bring many benefits. These include:

- the identification of problems and issues in your approach (many of which will be of a minor nature and can be speedily resolved).
- better understanding of client problems and needs.
- happier clients, who appreciate that you care about quality, are

listening to their views and are prepared to do something about them. This can considerably improve your chances of winning further work.

- a good general image throughout the organisation (which, again, can help you to win work with new clients).

Post-proposal surveys

Obtaining the views of clients following submission of a proposal, but before a project actually begins, can be a valuable means of finding out why a job was won or lost. Many external consulting firms carry out client surveys to gain this information and modify their approaches to marketing and proposal preparation accordingly.

Again, an interview with the client following a standard questionnaire format is the best way to find out detailed information. This is usually no problem when the proposal has been accepted and the job won, but there may be a certain reluctance to talk to you if your proposal has been rejected. Even in the internal consulting context where your clients are managers from the same organisation, a telephone interview or completion of a questionnaire form may be the only way to persuade the would-be client to give details.

In this case the interview need not be as long or detailed as a client satisfaction interview. The main two areas of questioning will be:

- why did we win/lose the work? Which particular aspects of our approach contributed most to our success/led to our rejection?
- was the work won/lost in competition with other tenderers (e.g. external consultancies)? If won, what singled us out from the competition? If lost, what did our competitors offer that we didn't?

Proposals are usually won because the client liked the overall approach, felt confident in the consultants ability to do the work and felt that they understood the key business issues. Cost is also frequently a major factor. Conversely, among the most common reasons given for rejection of a proposal are cost, insufficient experience, failure to convince the client of the benefits of the project and the belief that they, the client, are capable of doing the work themselves. These are all valid reasons – but there may be others which you will only establish by talking directly to the client. People who have turned you down for one reason or another have a tendency to feel embarrassed about it, and may be inclined to give a false response unless probed further: 'We liked your proposal, but you were too expensive/we felt on balance we can manage by ourselves'.

What benefits can post-proposal surveys bring? Above all, they can enable you to fine-tune your approach to winning work, based on the views of your clients and what they actually want. As with satisfaction surveys, you are also demonstrating your commitment to quality improvement and to listening to your clients' views. A further benefit is that you can identify the main channels and blockages, from an organisational point of view, to your winning consulting work. These might include the main sponsors of consultancy projects, the extent to which external consultants are invited to tender for work.

Implementation progress reviews

It can be instructive, once a reasonable period of time has elapsed following conclusion of a project and responsibility for continuing implementation has been handed over to the client, to assess the extent to which recommendations have proved to be of value. This demonstrates continued commitment to the client and a genuine interest in the results of recommendations made.

This may involve further interviews with your main client contact, but you should seek additional evidence of effective implementation of your recommendations and how people are coping with the new responsibilities or demands placed upon them. This evidence may be acquired in a number of ways:

- observing or interviewing client staff who are working with the changes you have recommended. How are they coping with the change? Is it easing their workload, or helping them in key aspects of their work? Have they encountered any problems that have caused them to postpone, abandon or adapt important areas of recommendation?
- reviewing hard data relating to performance improvement that can be ascribed to implementation of your recommendations (for

example: improved productivity figures, better response times, faster information processing, fewer customer complaints, lower staff turnover figures).

- approaching customers or users of the service provided by your client (these may be internal or external), to ascertain whether or not they perceive any service improvements since implementation of your recommendations. This is a key performance measure, although it can in some cases be difficult to ascertain whether improvements are due to your recommendations or not.

It can often happen that, on investigation, progress towards implementation has not been as rapid as you would have hoped and expected. This may be because your recommendations were wide of the mark, or simply because there is unwillingness amongst client staff to go through with a complex and difficult change process. If the latter, you should at the very least offer your views on how to facilitate change and make it more acceptable. This is a key aspect of your role as process consultant and change agent, and a demonstration of your commitment to your clients and to the success of the organisation as a whole.

IMPLEMENTING A QUALITY MANAGEMENT PROGRAMME

The quality measurement processes described in this chapter provide the building blocks' for a comprehensive quality management programme. This involves analysis of all information obtained and the implementation of positive measures to effect improvement where this is required. Quality management is absolutely essential for the internal consultant. You should regard it as a consulting project in its own right, the client in this case being yourself.

If you are a sole practitioner, you will have to do all the project work yourself. Otherwise, you should appoint one consultant from your internal consulting unit as quality manager, combining this role with his/her client responsibilities. This person must have the authority to carry out wide-ranging research, and implement all quality measures that are identified as necessary to improve the client service of the practice as a whole.

You should adopt a quality mission statement, which might be something like this:

'We are dedicated to giving clients an excellent service at all times, identifying their problems and meeting their needs through the provision of high-quality, professional consulting services. We will communicate with our clients on a continuing basis, to understand their needs better and improve the standard of our professional services.'

This mission statement should be the quality manager's *raison d'être*, reinforcing his/her role as the monitor and enforcer of professional consulting standards. The quality manager's role will encompass the following:

- carrying out the research and investigation methods described above – i.e. project quality reviews, client satisfaction surveys, post-proposal surveys, implementation progress reviews. The quality manager must have free rein to investigate any project undertaken by the consulting practice, including projects that are still in progress.
- analysing information obtained from research and defining methods of overcoming specific or general problems that reduce client service standards.
- giving feedback, recommendations and advice to consultants and to the practice leader. Much of this will concern specific problems of concern to the client that can easily be rectified. It will also include broader recommendations that apply to professional standards as a whole, requiring clearer definition of these standards. Advice given should not, however, be purely negative; where consultants are doing a good job this should be reinforced by positive feedback.
- ensuring implementation of recommendations. This may require the drawing up of detailed instructions or training for consultants, and ongoing review of service standards to ensure compliance.

The quality manager will need the full backing of the practice leader if he/she is to be effective in the role. There is always likely to be some friction with colleagues who may resent negative feedback and be reluctant to implement changes in their methods of working. It is a role requiring tact and diplomacy, as well as thorough investigative skills.

Project administration: BS5750

Efficient project administration should form a part of any quality management programme. Consultants and managers should be required to keep project files that are tidy and comprehensive to the extent that someone not involved in the work (such as the quality manager) can pick up the file and gain a clear picture of the nature and purposes of the project and the progress made. Information held in files should, at the very least, include:

- copies of the workplan, proposal, any other documents relating to the terms of reference and budgets.
- a list of all people interviewed, and copies of interview notes (this should include not just fact-finding interviews but other forms of meeting such as project start-up meetings).
- copies of correspondence and file notes of significant telephone conversations.
- copies of any hard data obtained or relevant reports, studies and other documents.
- copies of all client reports issued, presentation material used, implementation plans or other deliverables.
- records of time spent on the project, expenses and bills submitted.
- working notes – e.g. relating to analysis of data, development of recommendations, statistical charts or tables used to facilitate solution development.
- a formal record of the 'signing off' of the project.

Many external consultancies have implemented BS5750 as part of their drive to establish efficient project administration standards; in some cases also because key clients (notably in the public sector) are insisting on BS5750 before they are prepared to issue invitations to tender. BS5750 can, however, be a double-edged sword. It can involve an inordinate amount of administration; obtaining signatures for forms, maintaining records of all kinds of minutiae. It requires external assessors being given access to your records and files, to decide whether your standards are satisfactory or not (albeit these assessors are usually very helpful in rectifying matters that they regard as a requirement for qualification). It can be expensive, requiring input from external consultants and the costs of assessor visits and registration. Above all, it is entirely to do with internal administration and nothing to do directly with the quality of the consulting work you do for clients.

On the other hand; if the organisation as a whole is going for BS5750, you may be obliged to follow suit. It is possible that some or all of your clients – either internal or external – may require it. At the very least, because BS5750 is far from easy to achieve it demonstrates a commitment to quality that cannot be ignored and is therefore a strong selling point.

Whether you implement BS5750 or not, one thing you should certainly do is maintain a database of all work you have carried out. Completed project files should be held centrally, or archived once a suitable time period has elapsed (two to five years is suggested as a suitable time lapse before files are sent to archive). You should also keep a library of enquiries and proposals, even when these have not resulted in work won – they are invaluable reference points should a dormant enquiry reappear, or if you are subsequently approached by a different client for a similar piece of work. You should also maintain a summary database of all work carried out by all consultants in the practice, for ease of reference. This database should include:

- a brief resumé (one or two paragraphs) of the project;
- the names of the consultants involved;
- the dates on which the project started and finished;
- the value of the work in terms of time spent and fees;
- the file or archive reference number so full details can be accessed.

Professional ethics

Ethics and independence is a big issue for external consulting firms. It is important that consultants do not use information they obtain about clients to their personal advantage, and equally important to avoid conflicts brought about by consultants advising two or more clients who happen to be competitors. In most cases these considerations are less relevant to an internal consultant, but this does not mean that professional ethics can be ignored. On the contrary, your credibility depends on the maintenance of high standards. You need to ensure that you, and any other consultants within your practice, are clear as to what constitutes ethical behaviour and what they must do to abide by it.

This involves drawing up a code of ethics for the consultancy and ensuring this is widely understood (in many consulting practices this is another role for the quality manager). The code should encompass the following:

- integrity: consultants should not use underhand means to obtain information either from internal or external sources. They should be particularly careful in doing work for different parts of the organisation that are in conflict, and where advice given may deepen that conflict: in extreme cases, this may even mean turning potential work down. Consultants should not make recommendations from which they will obtain personal financial benefit (the opportunity for this may be rare, but may occur, for example, where the project involves selection of an external service supplier).
- confidentiality: consultants should not disclose information about projects to anyone other than the client and/or project sponsor, unless given leave to do so by the client. They must also adhere to standards of confidentiality in carrying out surveys involving external organisations, where a requirement for supplying information may be that the supplier is not identified.
- independence and objectivity: consultants should make recommendations that meet the client's **needs**. They should not be influenced by their own personal preferences, or select an option just because it is easier to recommend or is preferred by the client. Nor should they be influenced by what some other third party wants them to do.

- skill and competence: consultants should not embark on projects they are not qualified to do. They should seek assistance if there are any specific areas of work in a project for which they are not competent.
- care and diligence: consultants should exercise care and thoroughness in carrying out research, analysing data, developing recommendations and solutions. They should plan their work thoroughly and adhere to project plans, timescales and budgets as far as possible.

This may seem a formidable set of standards, but adhering to them should not be a problem for any consultant who is professional in approach and is prepared to recognise the demands and limitations of management consulting.

7

THE PROJECT THAT WENT WRONG. . . AND THE ONE THAT WENT RIGHT

This chapter is intended to provide graphic illustration of how an internal consulting project can fulfil its objectives or can go horribly wrong. The projects themselves are fictitious, but based on real experience: we know, because they happened to us. In the case of 'the project that went wrong' it may be suspected that some of the unfortunate consequences are exaggerated. While this is true in the round, each one of the individual errors made in the case study has, potentially, the scope to ruin the consultants' credibility and hence the whole project. We therefore make no apologies for our exaggeration.

THE PROJECT THAT WENT WRONG. . . THE LEADENHALL BANK

The main players in this sorry tale are Jim Plaistow, a newly-appointed consultant to the internal consulting unit of the bank; Willie Merton, a managing consultant in the unit; and Isabelle Ickenham, manager of the Investment Division back office.

The background

The bank had set up the consulting unit some two years previously, with the main objective of reviewing and improving the IT systems in use throughout its diverse business divisions. The unit had grown rapidly, now numbering twelve consultants of varying degrees of seniority, mostly with an IT background. Some consultants recruited to carry out specific projects were still doing the same work they had started on their first day with the consultancy; this helped to create an atmosphere in the practice of some general disillusionment. The practice was still expanding, however, and had recently started taking on consultants with more diverse backgrounds.

Jim Plaistow was the first consultant recruited into the practice with a marketing background. He had transferred over from the branch banking marketing department some six weeks before, and was already finding consulting tough going. He had little in common with other colleagues, who in the main were absorbed in their own project work. He had, as yet, received no training in what he was supposed to be doing. Above all, he had not as yet had any inkling of client work on the horizon. He found it difficult to resist the temptation to sneak off back to his old department from time to time, if only for a chinwag with his former colleagues.

One Monday afternoon, Jim was called in unexpectedly to see the head of the consulting practice. The conversation went something like this:

'Jim, good afternoon. I expect you've been finding things a little slow since you came over to us?'

Jim shuffled his feet a little nervously.

'Well, yes . . . I haven't actually been involved in any client work as yet. But I've been reading as much material about consulting as I can, and I'm building up contacts with quite a few people who I think might be interested in work in my field . . .'

'Yes . . . yes, that's very good. But I'm glad to say that something's come up in the Investment Division that you might be able to help with. Tell me: how much do you know about contracts?'

'Contracts? What – you mean with suppliers – advertising, office services, that sort of thing?'

'No, not exactly . . . well, I mean, yes . . . I mean, all contracts are more or less the same, you know.'

Jim was doubtful about this, but didn't like to say so.

'Yes . . . I suppose so . . . well, I've done some work on advertising contracts, you know, evaluating different proposals, drafting terms of reference . . .'

'Good. That sounds fine for the kind of work we want here. I'll tell Willie Merton you're OK for the job. He's the project manager. Can you phone him now, and go over to the Investment Division and see him as soon as possible?'

Jim rose to go. He didn't really have a clue about what he was being asked to do, but at any rate it was client work at last. He went back to his desk straight away and rang Willie Merton.

The initial briefing

Jim went over to see Willie Merton later that afternoon. He found him in a small, windowless office in the investment banking building, just a few blocks away. He didn't know Willie at all, having only seen him once or twice on the rare occasions Willie was in the consulting office; no one had bothered to introduce him. All Jim knew about him was that he was an IT consultant who had been managing a big project in investment banking for some time.

Willie, rather a self-contained man at the best of times, was particularly absorbed with his problems when Jim came to see him. He knew Jim didn't really have the background for the job he had in mind, but he was the only consultant available and he hoped could pick things up quickly. Willie had started the investment banking IT development project over a year before, he had already overshot on his budget and timescales, and the client was starting to ask questions about when things would be put right. Jim was a relatively cheap resource, could hopefully get to grips with an (albeit minor) part of the project, and was a visible demonstration to the client that he was responding to her needs.

'What I need you to do,' Willie began, *'is look through some custody agreements. Didn't Peter tell you it was about custody agreements? Well, doesn't matter; I've got some here for you to look at. If you ask*

around in the back office, you might find there's some more. Just look at them initially, and tell me what you think. What I'm after is finding out what's in them and what's missing from them; whether they're as comprehensive as they should be. Do you see?'

Jim didn't see, not at all, and though he didn't want to appear stupid he thought he'd better find out more before left to his own devices.

'I see what you want in general terms, but can you be more specific? Is there anything in particular I should look out for? Is there anything else I can read, you know, to find out what should be included?'

'Nothing specific, no; but don't worry, just give me your general impressions. Background reading; well, there's some of the project files on the shelf up there, you might familiarise yourself a little by looking through some of those.'

'OK, I'll do that . . . these are the agreements you have, are they? Well, I'll look through them, and then report back. By the way, how much time have you budgeted for this work?'

'Time? Oh, about twelve days should do for the whole project, you know, getting the information, putting it onto a spreadsheet, visiting the department and all that. . .but don't worry too much about the time. Look, I've got to go now, is there anything else you need to know?'

There were so many things Jim felt he needed to know that he started to panic. What was he actually supposed to be doing with the wretched agreements?

'Look, there's quite a few things . . . I mean . . . spreadsheets . . . you mentioned spreadsheets. I've never actually used spreadsheets before . . .'

'Oh, don't worry, they're easy enough to learn; you can do it in EXCEL. You don't know EXCEL? It's easy, as I said. Sandy, the project administrator, will show you. Look, if that's all, I've got to go now. Let me know if you have any problems. 'Bye then.'

Willie swept out of the room, leaving Jim feeling rather disconsolate and wholly confused. He still had no idea what he was required to do. Being a resourceful chap, however, he settled down and started to run through some of the custody agreements.

Early progress

Largely through his own initiative and resources, Jim gradually worked himself into the custody agreements project. Reading through some of the agreements Willie had given him as well as the few textbooks he found lying around, he acquired a vague understanding of terms that had initially been double Dutch to him: global custody, nostro and vostro accounts, correspondent banking. He took the opportunity of talking to some of the other consultants working in the Investment Division who, though they couldn't offer much practical help, at least provided moral support. Jim soon learned that the atmosphere generally around the office was not optimistic. However, he didn't let this worry him, and buckled down as well as he could to his task. He even gained a rudimentary knowledge of spreadsheets, so he was able to classify some of the information he found out.

He had spent a couple of weeks largely left to his own devices, and felt he had made some progress towards achieving what was expected of him. He did feel rather uneasy about the amount of time he was spending on research; after all, Willie had told him he had about twelve days to finish the project, and he had spent almost all of that time already. But overall, he thought things were going rather well. He had unearthed some useful material that he was sure Willie would find of interest.

His problems, however, really started from the time of his first progress meeting with Willie. It wasn't that Willie was particularly aggressive, or showed lack of appreciation about what he'd produced; but during the meeting Jim gradually began to realise the extent of what he still had to achieve.

'This material looks fine, for a first draft' Willie had begun, on looking through his spreadsheet. *'. . . though it'd be helpful if you*

added a couple of columns about reporting arrangements, service level agreements, that sort of thing. Have you talked to any of the section heads in the back office yet? One thing I really need to know is whether or not they have on-line facilities with any of these custodians. And what about alternative suppliers; you might talk to some of the other banks about their on-line facilities, what sort of links they have with their sub-custodians. And then when you've done that, you need to produce a summary of your recommendations so I can build them into the project report as a whole.'

Jim's spirits sank further and further the longer Willie spoke.

'But . . . I thought you said you just wanted me to look at the existing custody agreements? Classify the contents of them, and do you a report . . .'

'Why, yes, but I do need a bit more than that. Look, just go and talk to Isabelle Ickenham, get her to tell you what systems they're using in the back office, and point you in the direction of the section heads. Then go and talk to some alternative suppliers.'

'But . . . what about the budget? I've spent eight or nine days on this already . . . you said I only had twelve days.'

'Well, you'll just have to be careful with the time you've got left. Don't worry if you go a day or two over budget – the job can stand that. But you should be able to come up with something pretty quickly, if you talk to the right people in the back office . . .'

Jim went back to his desk with a heavy heart. If this was consulting, he wasn't so sure he was cut out for it.

Running into Problems

Jim managed to arrange a meeting with Isabelle Ickenham a couple of days later. She was a woman in her mid-forties who had worked for the bank for many years, and had acquired the reputation for being rather more strong-minded than the norm. Jim was aware of this, and went to the meeting well prepared.

'Thanks for agreeing to see me at such short notice,' he began, *'I just*

wanted to put you in the picture about how my particular part of the IT project is going, and agree with you what steps I need to take to progress things further. As you know, I've been looking at your custody agreements, and I know you're thinking about reviewing the levels of service you receive from your custodians . . .'

Isabelle Ickenham cut him short.

'Do you know that? Well, it's news to me. I know we use a lot of custodians, but that's essential given our position in the market. Generally I'm very happy about the levels of service we receive.'

*'But . . . you **are** looking at having better on-line facilities, aren't you? At least, that's what Willie Merton said . . .'*

'Willie Merton said! I don't really care what Willie Merton said; or, at least, I wish he'd say it to me. I haven't seen him for nearly two weeks.' She snorted contemptuously. *'Frankly, I don't think he knows what he's doing any more. I was hoping by now he'd have come up with a set of proposals for a complete review of our IT systems. Instead of which I get this – global custody agreements!'*

Jim smiled at her weakly. His preparation for the meeting was already shot to pieces. He didn't have a clue what to say. Fortunately, Isabelle Ickenham saved him.

'I'm sorry – I know I'm a bit brusque sometimes – I know it's not your fault' she continued, *'but really it does annoy me that I'm not kept aware of what's going on. This project never seems to have got off the ground, and things are going from bad to worse.'*

She stood up from her desk, and began pacing about the room.

'Look, I suppose it might be quite useful to find out what kind of on-line facilities are available now. Why don't you talk to some of my section heads about it?'

Jim agreed that this was what he had in mind.

'Good. I'm sure they'll tell you about their requirements. You're familiar with custody enquiry and reporting systems, I suppose?'

'Well, not exactly; but I expect they're fairly easy to come to terms with.'

'Hmm . . . they are a bit specialised, you know. But you know about the basic software packages we use in the back office, at any rate?'

'To some extent, yes . . . I mean, in general terms . . . I'm really from a marketing background, you see . . .'

Isabelle Ickenham stopped marching round the room, and stared hard at him. As soon as he had gone, she picked up the phone and rang Willie Merton.

The outcome

The immediate outcome was an angry meeting between Isabelle Ickenham and Willie Merton. This didn't exactly progress matters further, but at the end of it each of them knew where they stood. In Willie's case this was 'In trouble with the Head of the Consulting Practice'.

The project wasn't cancelled, but within a few days Willie was replaced as project manager by another of his colleagues from the practice. All consultants working on the project were required to provide him with a brief concerning the work they were doing. It became apparent from this that co-ordination of the work was minimal, communication between different consultants non-existent, and the original workplan (such as it was, Willie's style being to rely on a few pages of handwritten and almost indecipherable notes) hugely at odds with what Isabelle Ickenham had said she wanted. Discussing things further with the Head of the Practice, the new project manager decided on a damage limitation exercise.

As far as Jim Plaistow was concerned, he was told to complete his research as quickly as possible and present his findings to the project manager in a summary report. He understood perfectly well by now that this was just a token attempt to validate the exercise. He interviewed three or four of the back office section heads, finding them generally lacking any interest in reporting systems and perfectly satisfied with what they had already. He visited a couple of suppliers, only to be blinded by their demonstrations of all-singing, all-dancing software packages and their hard-sell attitudes (he was pestered by them afterwards for weeks, in the hope that they could sell him something). He prepared a report that received little critical comment or amendment, though only a brief summary of it appeared in the overall project report (rather grandly called the IT Improvement Project Implementation Plan). Six months later, this report was still sitting on the shelf in Isabelle Ickenham's office.

Jim felt thoroughly disillusioned by his introduction to internal consulting. Three months later, as the work of the consulting unit slackened off – largely as a result of the poor reports that spread through the bank about it concerning the investment banking IT development project – he returned to the marketing department. Consulting, he had decided, was not for him.

What went wrong

This piece of work – both the IT development project as a whole and Jim Plaistow's involvement in it – was so fraught with problems and weaknesses that we have little doubt the reader will have spotted many of them. Overall, it illustrates the sort of rapid downwards spiral that can occur if a project is badly managed and the consultants working on it poorly prepared.

Project management

Looking first at the project management, it is abundantly clear that Willie Merton sadly neglected his responsibilities in this area. In particular:

- Willie clearly made little attempt to understand his client's needs: Jim's conversation with Isabelle Ickenham alone reveals that he had simply not done enough research in this area. Global custody agreements, the specific project in which Jim was concerned, is an example of an area that did not feature at all in Isabelle's mind as something needing investigation.
- this conversation also reveals the lack of communication between

Willie and Isabelle Ickenham throughout the project. A key aspect of the project manager's role is to maintain contact with the client on a regular basis, reporting on progress and ensuring the client's needs are continuing to be met. This did not take place during this project.

- no proper workplan was prepared prior to commencement. As a result, Willie had no benchmark against which to compare the progress made by his consultants, and timescales and budgets were allowed to overrun.
- the briefing given to Jim was vague and misleading. At no time was Jim told exactly what his objectives were, the steps he should take to achieve his objectives and the precise amount of time he had at his disposal. Following their initial conversation, Willie was not readily available to Jim to help him with problems and queries. He was unresponsive to the fact that Jim knew next to nothing about custody agreements; even Jim's misgivings concerning his poor knowledge of EXCEL were dismissed offhandedly.

Overall, much of the blame for the failure of the project must be laid at Willie's door. As project manager, he was responsible for planning, control and reporting to the client. None of these crucial areas was addressed properly.

Jim Plaistow

However, there are also things that Jim could have done differently. He was in a difficult position: new to the consulting practice, asked to do a piece of work for which he was clearly not suited, not wanting to appear negative or unwilling to become involved in client work. But in retrospect, it would have been far better for him to have told the Head of the Consulting Practice right at the beginning that he could not do the project.

Having become involved, Jim should have been firmer in his dealings with Willie Merton concerning the latter's expectations of him. He should not have accepted Willie's vagueness about the work required. He should have been more proactive in seeking him out when he was unsure of what to do next. Had he done so, he might have managed his own time better (for instance, by going to see Isabelle Ickenham rather sooner than he did, in order to ascertain her views and follow up her advice).

The consulting environment

Finally, there were several aspects of the way the internal consulting practice was run that contributed to the problems encountered:

- it was madness to allow a consultant like Jim Plaistow, with no experience of IT, to become involved in an IT project. From the perspective of the project itself, he was clearly not capable of doing the work properly. Taking a wider perspective, the risk to the reputation of a practice brought about by making inappropriate use of consultants' skills is simply too high to be taken.
- to compound this, Jim was given no initial training in professional consulting skills, or the role of the consultancy within the bank as a whole. He was simply expected to find his own feet as best he could, and with minimal support from his new colleagues.
- the practice as a whole had no mission statement, defined objectives, or quality control systems. It had grown rapidly but without taking shape or direction. It responded to the perceived requirements of its clients, rather than being proactive in defining client needs and responding to these in the context of the strategic direction of the bank. Little wonder, therefore, that under these circumstances it became involved in a project that was allowed to drift so aimlessly.

THE PROJECT THAT WENT RIGHT . . . SPORTS AND LEISURE PUBLICATIONS LTD.

The scenario here concerns one Sophie Clerkenwell, a consultant in the internal practice of a large conglomerate with interests in many commercial fields.

The conglomerate operated on a holding company basis, and had set up a consulting group within the holding company itself to provide a service to its subsidiaries. The group had remained small, only five consultants in all; each with different professional skills and backgrounds. Consultants were encouraged to communicate directly with the subsidiary companies, establishing contacts and finding work for themselves and their colleagues. Following initial training in basic consulting skills, they were expected to be independent thinking in their approach, but to work effectively as a team when appropriate. The structure worked well: morale was high, the consultants worked well together in establishing leads and making use of their multidisciplinary skills in carrying out client work.

The background

Sophie's particular specialist area was human resources management, training and organisation development. One day, she was contacted by one of her colleagues, Tony Wanstead, a financial management specialist who had been working for some time in the company's magazine publishing subsidiary.

> *'Hello, Sophie'* Tony began, *'d'you remember that meeting we had about two months ago with the Managing Director of Sports and Leisure Publications? You know, when we talked about writing a personnel manual setting out all the terms and conditions? Well, he mentioned it to me again yesterday.'*

Sophie tried to recall the details of the meeting. As far as she could remember, the Managing Director's interest had been aroused by one of the consultancy's brochures that Tony had given him, and he had expressed some interest in a personnel manual. He appeared fairly lukewarm about it at the time, she seemed to remember.

> *'I don't think he was all that interested then, and I didn't want to keep pestering him about it. But he's had one or two staff problems recently, particularly with the typesetters, and so I thought it might be worth reminding him. He seems much keener on the idea now. Do you think you could come over and talk to him again about it?'*

The upshot of this conversation was a further meeting between Sophie, Tony and the Managing Director, two days later. Sophie had used the intervening time to prepare a few ideas for the discussion, and find out as much as she could about the magazine publishing subsidiary. As far as she could tell it was doing quite well, but had recently modernised its typesetting processes with some resultant redundancies amongst staff.

After introducing Sophie, Tony left her with the Managing Director to discuss the details of the potential work. The Managing Director, though more positive than he had been before, was still doubtful.

'You see, I'm sure it would be useful to have a proper manual', he mused, *'in which everything is set down in one place so that people know where they stand. But I'm not sure how it would, directly, overcome the sort of problems we have at present: you know, rumblings of discontent following the redundancies, complaints about the training required to operate the new computerised type-setting processes . . .'*

'I wouldn't begin to pretend that having a personnel manual will overcome all your problems', Sophie interposed. *'But surely, if all your expectations of staff, and all the terms and conditions, were put in one manual, people would be happier about where they stood. Take training as an example; the training courses are available, aren't they?'*

'Well, yes, they're available . . . but the typesetters just bang on about not being able to go on them. It's as if they didn't know we've set up the courses specifically to help them . . .'

'So clearly, there's a communication problem you've got on your hands. Surely, having a personnel manual would help overcome that? Not completely, of course, but surely an important step in the right direction . . .'

By gradual degrees, Sophie began to convince the Managing Director that having a personnel manual could indeed go a long way towards solving some of his problems. At the end of the meeting, they had agreed she would prepare a proposal setting out how she would produce one, including the costs and timescales involved.

Smooth progress early on

Sophie spent the whole of the next day on her proposal. Initially, she developed a workplan in which she built in time for the required amount of desk research, fact-finding and other interviews, the development and presentation of recommendations. She also allowed for a series of progress meetings with the Managing Director, and a certain amount of input from Tony Wanstead. She correctly felt that his understanding of the client would be invaluable, particularly in the early stages of the project. Overall, Sophie estimated that five weeks' work would be required to complete the project, over a lapsed timescale of two months.

The proposal itself took the form of a four-page letter to the Managing Director, setting out the stages in the work programme, the inputs required from the Managing Director and his Administration Manager, the reporting arrangements, costs and timescales and the deliverables. It also reiterated the benefits to be gained from preparation and issue to all staff of a comprehensive personnel manual.

Sophie posted the proposal letter to the Managing Director, and two days later went to see him about it. The outcome was that, following some further discussion concerning details of the approach and the level of support required from the Administration Manager, the proposal was accepted without amendment. Sophie started work straight away.

Initially, things went according to plan. With the help of the Administration Manager, Sophie was able to gain access to all the people within the magazine publishing company she wished to see, and soon accumulated all the background information she needed. She began the process of outlining the content and format of the manual, and gained agreement to this from the Managing Director at progress meetings. Her costings and timescales had proved accurate, so far. She moved into the second stage of the project, preparation of the first draft of the manual. Pretty soon she had a version that she felt was complete enough to discuss with the Managing Director.

A problem overcome

At Sophie's meeting with the Managing Director to discuss her draft manual, everything at first went fine. He seemed more than pleased with the progress she had made, and the style and content of the manual. They debated one or two areas where minor changes might be made. Then the Managing Director dropped his bombshell.

> *'As you know, I'm very satisfied with the work you've done,'* he began, *'and subject to the changes we've agreed I'm sure we can finalise the manual and have it circulated. There's just one thing though . . .'* he began leafing through the draft, looking for a section somewhere in the middle, *'ah, yes, here it is. This section on redundancy terms . . .'*

> *'Redundancy terms? Oh, yes, I understand you've had a redundancy agreement for several years, so I've incorporated it into the manual . . .'*

> *'Well yes, that's the point. What it is, I've been thinking of changing the redundancy agreement. On the whole, I think it's a bit too generous. I wonder if you could just tone it down a little, you know, make it closer to the ordinary statutory terms than it is now. . .'*

Sophie drew a deep breath. Tony had told her the Managing Director had a tendency to strike off at a tangent, and that when he did it could be very difficult to deflect him from his purpose. This was the first time however that Sophie had experienced this tendency, and she knew she could not agree to what he wanted. In the first place, drawing up new employment conditions wasn't part of the terms of reference of the project. More importantly, she foresaw all kinds of problems if redundancy clauses were changed unilaterally. It would be a blatant breach of employment contracts. The typesetters in particular, she knew, would be up in arms about it. It would, furthermore, totally discredit the production of the personnel manual, which would be seen not as a means of communicating better with the staff but an underhand way of reducing their terms and conditions of employment. She decided to confront the issue head on.

> *'I'm sorry – but I really don't think it would be a good idea to use the*

personnel manual to change terms and conditions,' she began, *'you see, you can't just make amendments to the contract without people having agreed to it first; that would be breach of contract.'*

The Managing Director waved her comments airily aside.

*'Oh, I know, Pat Shepherd's told me all about that. But I don't suppose anyone would notice. The redundancy terms are buried deep inside the manual. After all, it's not as if there's any intention to actually **make** any more staff redundant.'*

'So – if that's the case, what do you want to change the redundancy agreement for?'

'Well you never know, do you? Maybe, in two or three years' time, if further changes take place, we may need some further staff cutbacks . . .'

Sophie decided to stand her ground.

'Look, I'm sorry as I said, but I'm not prepared to build in a fundamental change to terms and conditions like that. Even if staff don't spot the changes immediately – and there's no guarantee that they won't – it's bound to come to light sooner or later. Just think of the adverse effect on morale that would have, particularly as you've just had quite a few redundancies! And anyway, ultimately you'd have to pay staff according to the original terms – any industrial tribunal would see it immediately as a breach of contract, so you'd be faced with tribunal costs as well as the actual payments. No, it's not on; if you want to change the redundancy agreement, you'll have to do it the proper way.'

The Managing Director shuffled awkwardly on his seat.

'The proper way? And what exactly would that be, in your opinion?' he grumbled.

'Well, you'd have to negotiate the changes. Maybe you could get your existing staff to accept them, or maybe not. You could still introduce a different agreement for new staff – bring in change that way. That's how I'd go about it.'

'Would you? Well, maybe you're right – it's something else for the future.'

Sophie breathed a sigh of relief. The project was back on course.

Towards successful conclusion

From this point on, things continued smoothly as before. The further drafts of the personnel manual that Sophie prepared were accepted by the Managing Director and his top management team, the finally agreed version was printed and circulated to staff throughout the company. The project had been completed within timescale and budget, all deliverables had been met, and the Managing Director seemed pleased with the overall result.

At the final debriefing meeting, Sophie asked the Managing Director if he felt the project had met its objectives.

'Well yes, on the whole,' he replied, *'as you know my main aim was to let people know where they stand, give them confidence, settle them down after the period of upheaval we've just been through. I think issuing the manual has certainly helped with that. And in addition it has certainly proved instructive to me to have at my fingertips all these details about terms and conditions that I never knew existed.'*

'So, do you think it'll help create a better atmosphere throughout the business?'

'Yes – yes, I do – in fact, I think it already has. I know people are reading the manual. I think in some cases they've discovered things – benefits, that is – that they didn't really know about. I've always believed in open communication, and this manual is certainly proving to be a good way of communicating with people.'

Sophie wasn't too sure, based on her experience of dealing with him, whether 'open communication' really was part of the Managing Director's style. However, she let the point rest.

'In view of the way the project went,' she continued, *'was there anything I did that you think I should have done differently?'*

The Managing Director reflected for a minute, then chuckled to himself.

'No, I don't think so – I'm not sure I thought that at the time though – I'm still a bit wary of dealing with consultants. You certainly took me aback when we were talking about redundancy agreements, but I can see now that you were right in the end. Talking of which, now the personnel manual's put to bed, that is an area I'd like you to help me with . . .'

Why the project was successful

This project was successful for a number of reasons. These include the thorough preparation that was carried out, the systematic way in which the work programme was managed and executed, and last but not least the general atmosphere and environment within the consulting group as a whole.

Consulting group environment

A range of specific factors have contributed to the creation of a cohesive, proactive consulting environment in which potential projects can be quickly identified and turned into 'won work'. These factors include:

- sound consulting skills training being given to all new consultants joining the group.
- effective use being made of the technical skills of individual consultants: Sophie Clerkenwell's background in human resources and training, for example, meant that she had ideal skills to carry out the project described in the case study. She would not have been expected to consult in areas outside the range of her expertise.
- effective networking and following up of leads: note that the leisure publishing project came about as a result of a lead established several months earlier. Through following up this lead at the appropriate time, Tony was able to convert it into a more definite enquiry and, ultimately, a project won.

- good teamworking: in this case between Tony Wanstead and Sophie Clerkenwell. Although specialising in different areas, Tony was able to identify an opportunity for Sophie, and the two of them worked together initially in approaching the client.
- consultants are encouraged to be independent-minded and pro-active: Sophie was given the freedom to respond quickly to the enquiry, meet the client, draw up terms of reference and manage her project to its conclusion.

Project planning

This project was planned thoroughly. At the initial meeting, Sophie was careful to explore, identify and clarify her client's needs. She explained how the work proposed could meet those needs, and why her skills enabled her to do the work.

Sophie prepared a thorough workplan, and from this developed a proposal that covered all the key aspects of the project (work to be done, work stages, objectives, costs, timescales etc.). It also identified the **benefits** to be gained from the work.

The proposal was in the form of a four-page letter, easy to read and digest. She met the client again following submission of the proposal letter, to clarify the approach suggested, make any modifications required to the workplan and ensure that the client's needs were met.

Sophie adopted a sound methodology in putting together her workplan. Features of this included:

- a comprehensive interview programme;
- sufficient time allowed for development of recommendations;
- involvement of a client counterpart (the Administration Manager) in the work;
- periodic reporting on progress and to ensure client needs were continuing to be met;
- a 'sign off' interview to bring the project to a formal conclusion.

Project management and execution

A key factor here was that Sophie stuck to her workplan: monitoring her progress and her budgets, and assessing client satisfaction continuously through the regular progress meetings. At no time did the project stray from its terms of reference or lose its sense of purpose in the way the Leadenhall Bank project did.

A further critical factor was the way that Sophie confronted problems that arose rather than avoiding them. We would not pretend that all problems encountered during a consulting engagement can be as simply overcome as the redundancy agreements issue faced by Sophie Clerkenwell – only too frequently, they can run on for days or even weeks before being resolved. However, the **approach** Sophie took is illustrative: she addressed the Managing Director's request directly but diplomatically, by explaining to him how it would produce effects directly contrary to his needs, and furthermore could prove extremely costly. In conscience, she could not have gone along with his request as it would have been both unethical and outside the terms of reference of her project. Many consultants, however, would have found it difficult to respond directly and would have been tempted to fudge the issue.

Overall, the project was successful because it met its terms of reference and the client's needs. There was strong evidence to suggest that it was being implemented, and was having beneficial effects throughout the organisation. This, ultimately, is the crucial test for a consulting project.

8

USING OTHER CONSULTANTS SUCCESSFULLY

Increasingly complex issues are necessitating the use of mixed teams of consultants. In many situations an established internal consultant may play a lead role in guiding the organisation in both choice and use of external consultants, but getting what you require may sometimes be troublesome. This chapter explores some key aspects of choice and suggests ways in which the selection process can be made as risk-free as possible.

Do you really need them?

There may be a number of reasons to hire-in consultants. They include

- the demands that a particular project will make cannot be fulfilled using in-house expertise.
- on a large project you may need additional resources but are unsure if this is a one-off occasion and would prefer to use 'temporary' consultants rather than add to your full-time team.
- as part of the development of your in-house services you may wish to 'learn' a new approach or methodology by having a consultant work with you and, by 'parallel running' add to your own repertoire for 'next time'.
- some projects require **complete** independence, hence the need for outside assistance.

WHAT TO LOOK FOR IN AN EXTERNAL CONSULTANT

Hopefully this book has identified those aspects of consulting which differentiate superior from indifferent performance. There are a number of ways these can be checked out.

Track record

Just as many employers fail to take up references on potential new hires, so do many companies fail to follow up references for potential consultants. There are a number of reasons for this – 'they were very plausible at the conference we attended . . . there just didn't seem any need', 'we just never got round to it . . . their first few weeks on site went well . . .', 'the Chairman had heard of them before so we didn't see the point'. Yet how many of us would buy a new car without a test-drive? It pays to check out the following:

- track record – has the consultancy done similiar work in your sector and when was the work performed? One prestigious client in a brochure may indicate nothing more than an individual attending a workshop on a completely different subject.
- is what you see what you get – other clients can give you an invaluable insight into the *modus operandi* of consultants:
  – how did they behave?
  – did they meet deadlines?
  – were their invoices accurate?
  – did they do what they said they would do?
  – how responsive were they to the organisational culture?
  – was the project a 'success'?
  – did they provide value for money?
  – would you use them again?
  – how competent were the individuals?
  – with hindsight did you need consultants at all?
  – on reflection was the project the right one?

Questions such as these provide a real insight into what actually happened during a consulting project. Whilst it would be unreasonable to expect perfection in every aspect, how difficulties encountered were overcome can be very revealing:

'Although we (the client) were the cause of a number of delays by hauling people off a working group at very short notice, they (the consultants) adjusted their schedule in consultation with ourselves and brought the project in on time, if a little over budget.'

'A major problem for us was lack of continuity, it was as if our job was second division stuff. What they seemed to forget was that to us it was the key job of the year.'

As in any other service industry 'moments of truth matter'. A reliable and professional practice will guard its reputation jealously and should be ready and willing to provide references.

Conferences, exhibitions etc.

Consultants are only too happy to present their approach to conferences. Some of these are mounted by the consultants themselves, while in other cases they are organised by professional conference organisers. Others are somewhat more independent, organised by professional bodies. Such occasions will always be viewed by consultants as a selling opportunity and they will seek to present themselves in the best light. But events such as these do give you the opportunity to take a look at a particular consultant's approach.

Notwithstanding this, conferences do tend to be dominated by the larger firms. Trade exhibitions on the other hand may be attended by a mix of consultancies: large and small. Again they provide an opportunity to meet potential providers face to face.

'BEAUTY PARADES': SELECTING YOUR CONSULTANT

Just as references may not be taken up, so may a client choose a consultant solely on opportunistic criteria: 'they sent us a mail-shot on the off-chance that we might be interested – we were, it was just what we wanted!' Things are changing however and some Government agencies now invite consultants to express interest in projects via advertisements in the press. The well-established alternative is some form of beauty parade – i.e. a process designed to enable a range of potential consultants to be viewed against a predetermined specification. Such an approach is reasonably efficient in time and allows key decision makers to get together and agree on a choice.

The normal format of this approach is to draw up terms of reference and invite a range of potential providers to discuss these with you. Two aspects of this are:

- how do you decide whom to invite? If you are new to consulting your knowledge may be sparse. If so, ask around your own professional network for ideas on possible providers and consult one of the annual guides to consulting.
- how do you provide further information? The issue here is who is managing the process – you or other consultants? You may wish to make yourself available whenever a potential collaborator wishes. Indeed in your early days this may be a very good means of testing out the skills and 'fit' of other consultants. Those with a clearer idea of the composition of a likely 'long list' may want to arrange a half day briefing for the long list collectively. This is very time effective from your point of view and appears to be an increasing trend.
- proposals should initially be reviewed against your specified requirements. What may sometimes emerge is an 'off the wall' approach which no one had contemplated. If this has any merit you may wish to include this as an outside chance along with the best three or four proposals. Chapter Three specifies the content of a proposal and this provides a useful checklist for this purpose:
  – anticipated scope of the project;
  – their approach and who will do the work;
  – progress measures;
  – experience of the project team;
  – timescales and costs;
  – deliverables and benefit.

SPECIFYING YOUR REQUIREMENTS

We opened this book with some thoughts on the distinction between what you want, what the consultant is offering and what you may actually need. An internal consultant is ideally placed to ensure that actual needs are focused upon, but on occasions it will undoubtedly be helpful to use discussions with potential providers to refine actual requirements. In any event it is important to be able to identify what is required against the following criteria:

- a description of the project, including context – i.e. why this project at this time;
- time frame, time constraints;
- extent of support available from within the organisation;
- budgetary implications;
- what the project will lead to:
  - report;
  - recommendations;
  - implementation.

One issue which needs careful thought is the extent to which you are prepared to share with potential providers your feel for the budget required to conduct the assignment.

INTERPRETING CONSULTANT-SPEAK AND OTHER INDICATORS

The previous sections specify the questions you need to address if you are to get value for money and a professional approach. However, there are a number of things to watch out for in a proposal or presentation.

Who, when

Who will be working with you? If you engage a sole practitioner to assist you, then obviously who you see is who you get. However, if you are talking to a large firm be alert to proposals that are vague about exactly who they will be providing to assist you. You must insist on meeting the individual(s) involved and on being given a copy of their CV. Have no qualms about testing them out. If they cannot satisfy you, they will probably not impress your client either.

Also watch out for the magic words 'subject to availability'. Obviously all consultants aim to maximise their earnings. Many will apply the taxi-rank principle of waiting for clients on a first come first served basis. If your selection process takes longer than you expect, you may find your preferred consultant is unavailable.

Ambiguity

One reason clients hire consultants is for their expertise. It follows therefore that they may well possess knowledge, skills, and 'know-how' in excess of your own. However, as we noted earlier, if something cannot be measured it cannot be managed. Consequently in a project requiring the application of a particular methodology, software, or analytical technique you must be clear about your own needs and whether the consultants who will be assisting you can actually 'deliver'. Once again, checking on their track record may prove invaluable in judging this.

Cost

Unfortunately, some consultants are deliberately vague about costs and fees. Beware of any that hedge their bets. Thus a proposal suggesting 'we anticipate this work will take us between 30 to 50 days at an average fee rate of £1,000 per day' is of little value to you. Ask for a detailed breakdown of fees relating to tasks and the staff involved. If this is not forthcoming look elsewhere for assistance.

Something else to be very clear about is the provision of facilities and the costs of support services. Some consultancy teams bring a secretary with them to prepare presentations etc. and make no demands upon your support resources. Others will ask for access to secretarial assistance. Should this not be forthcoming you may find yourself billed for typing and presentation preparation.

What will you get for your money?

A related area is what exactly will be delivered. In the case of the use of an outside 'expert' the deliverable may be what they contribute to the project by virtue of their skills and their input to, say, a report. But what about the use of software? Or a particular – and proprietary – approach to training. It may be that not only will you have to pay for advice during the project but subsequently a percentage – or some other on-cost – every time the material or approach is used in the future.

Check out licensing or copyright issues very carefully.

Arrange a demonstration

At some point in the selection process you must ensure that you have an adequate feel for the way in which the consultants will behave. Thus if you are engaging consultants to conduct training and development activities watch them doing some – either with an existing client or a run-through of their approach with a number of colleagues chosen by yourself. If the task involves, say, the use of Activity Based Costing give the consultant enough information in advance of your meeting to enable you to test them out.

ENSURING DELIVERY TO YOUR REQUIREMENTS RATHER THAN THE CONSULTANTS'

If you follow the steps outlined in this book then hopefully delivery will meet your own requirements. Many of the techniques set out in Chapters Three to Five apply to your relationship with, and management of, external consultants, For example:

- the importance of communication and regular progress meetings;
- the management of counterpart staff;
- continuous reference to your terms of reference.

However, you must continually remind yourself that in this context you are the client. There are two schools of thought on this aspect, one is that as a consultant yourself you will be a hard negotiator who will be difficult to please, a poacher turned gamekeeper, if you like. The other perspective is that you will much more readily empathise with your sub-contracted consultants in terms of a common professional bond. The truth is probably somewhere in the middle. But be warned, you must treat the relationship in a professional manner and not lower your own standards because the consultant you have engaged is an old friend who may 'need a helping hand'. Shaking hands on a deal without written terms of reference will cause major problems and may even end your friendship. So be crystal clear about what will be delivered by when. The choice of the right 'sub-contractor' should mean a high quality professional approach.

Who chooses?

Depending on the circumstances and the size of your organisation a large number of projects may be undertaken by external consultants. You may wish to position yourself as the reference point for information on what is available in the marketplace and to make yourself available to assist senior managers in the selection process. In part this will depend on your strategy. If your plan is to become the focus of all internal consulting then you will need to remind senior managers that you are ready, willing and able to help. Chapter Nine looks at this aspect in more depth.

9

MAKING THIS BOOK WORK FOR YOU

Having read this book you may have decided that internal consulting is not for you. Hopefully though, we will have excited interest and intellectual curiosity in the role of internal consultant. This chapter therefore looks at four aspects: have you got what it takes as an individual; is there a market for your skills; how can you develop an action plan for the future? And finally, we offer some observations on getting started.

ABOUT YOURSELF

Why are you reading this book? Perhaps because you want to become an internal consultant; maybe you are an internal consultant and want to take a fresh look; maybe you are thinking of creating an internal consulting unit; or maybe you are fed up with external consultants and want to understand more about how to manage them and get value for money.

Whatever your perspective or intention this book is very much a starting point.

Self-awareness

If you **are** thinking of a career move the following framework will get you to review some questions crucial to any career decision. If you wish you can jot down your thoughts and then review them. Another potentially more powerful way is to get your partner or a colleague who knows you pretty well to interview you using the questions below and to describe to you how they see you.

- Think about your career from the time you started work. How did you get to where you are today? Was it planned – premeditated – or did you just 'get lucky'.

The purpose here is to get you to review your approach to career management. If you just wait for things to happen, consulting is not for you.

- What are your competencies and areas of expertise? One way to do this is to describe your qualities, your behaviour, and your 'know-how'. How did you pick up your skills – through formal education/training? What are you good at? Equally how do you 'show up'? If your boss and your team had to describe you would they see a side of you that you don't?

Think about the key qualities of effective consultants – do you seem to possess them? If so, what examples are there in your career of 'making a difference'. If not, can training provide the answer?

- Review the examples and case material in this book – how would you have behaved in the circumstances outlined?
- What are your likes and dislikes?

Think very carefully about these responses. Are you persuading yourself that internal consulting is a soft option – somewhere out of the firing line? Or are you intent on developing a profit centre within your organisation? Would you enjoy working by yourself in what would effectively be a business start-up? Think about why clients hire consultants; do you *like* these activities: providing independent and unbiased judgement; presenting new ideas and a fresh approach. Do you enjoy diagnosing problems and evaluating possible solutions?

WHERE ARE YOU GOING?

- What would you like to be doing in five years time? Now answer the question again. Be open – be as ambitious as you dare. And describe why your position five years on will be satisfying to you.

The intention here is to get you to explore – in detail – what you want – not just in work terms but in the context of your life. So think about the impact of your ambition in the widest sense on your family and social life.

MAKING IT HAPPEN

- In the light of your previous answers what do you need to make happen to get where you want to be?

Who do you need to convince? How can people help/hinder you? What will be the rewards? What are the likely sacrifices?

How to acquire the skills

Making it happen involves a number of elements, in particular whether you have the right skills mix. In the light of your assessment you will have a feel for the extent to which you have the full range of skills required for internal consultant. In truth most of us will have entered the consultancy profession without experience in every aspect of the work. Many successful consultants will have started their careers with very limited exposure to selling, for example. Equally an experienced project manager from an IT background may have never been given any formal skills training in delivering present-ations.

There are a number of ways in which you can acquire and develop the requisite skills ranging from self-help to formal instruction:

Training courses

Many organisations run training courses in such areas as presentation skills and report writing. As with the choice of any training, ensure that you check out the relevance and quality of what is on offer. Cost will be another consideration. High-quality, one-to-one presentation skills training could cost a substantial sum. The matrix shown in Fig. 9.1 should help you to identify those areas where needs exist.

What	Your performance level				
	Low				High
Planning and conducting surveys					
Structured interviews					
Presentation skills					
Report writing					
Project management					
Coaching skills					
Problem solving					
Managing change					
Managing meetings					
Marketing skills					

Fig. 9.1 Personal skill levels assessment form

Rate yourself against the skills indicated, and indeed others relevant to your own situation. Be realistic about your current level of skill and rate yourself on the high/low scale. A high skills level would be characterised by relevant, recent training in the skill, reinforced by frequent opportunities to practise it. A low skills level would be indicated by both an absence of formal training and few opportunities to practise or observe the skill being used. If you position yourself somewhere in the mid-range this is likely to be characterised by some training but little opportunity to practise the skill or get feedback upon its application.

It may well be that a number of these skills are increasingly significant in the context of your current role so do not ignore the possibility of enhancing your skills in the context of your current job.

Observation

Rather less obvious and more difficult to arrange would be to get yourself involved as a 'shadow' on a consulting project in your own organisation. First reactions from both the external consultants and their internal client may be sceptical at first. Concerns about carrying a supernumerary on the project, and safeguarding confidentiality with an 'outsider' involved, are likely to be dominant. Getting yourself involved will be a real test of your influencing skills.

Working with consultants on a project

Rather than playing a passive role as observer there may be opportunities in your organisation to get fully involved as part of a project team. Here the maxim is 'if you don't ask you don't get'. Use your internal network to discover whether any projects are on the stocks and discuss with your boss the possibility and opportunity of getting involved.

As more organisations recognise the importance of getting their own people developed as part of a consultancy project to enable the organisation to sustain change in the future, these roles are increasing.

Talk to other consultants

Why not develop your networking expertise by targeting a number of consultancies – large and small – whose services seem to be aligned with what you would like to offer. Write to them explaining you are interested in getting an insight into the consulting process with a view to developing in-house expertise and would welcome the opportunity for a discussion. They are unlikely to turn you down – after all, you may be a future customer.

Developing your own personal development plan

A theme recurring throughout this book has been the importance of planning. If you do not plan what skills you need to acquire and by what means, you will not achieve your objectives. So identify a personal development plan to help you specify and achieve your goals. It doesn't need to take the form of an immaculately presented report, rather a working document covering the following:

- what skills do I need to acquire?
- what are the opportunities available to me for their acquisition – e.g. project work, training course?
- how will I be able to practise my skills and how will I be able to get feedback on my performance?
- who can help me acquire and practise these skills?

Be realistic and develop a plan covering the next six months. Track your progress on a fortnightly basis and at the end of the period review progress against the plan. If you are on track all well and good, if not why not? What has thwarted you? Was your plan untenable?

- has poor time management been the cause?
- do you lack the necessary self discipline?
- have your priorities shifted?

In the light of this analysis you will need to reconfirm your intentions or choose another route.

Focusing on what it might mean

One useful way of thinking about what being a consultant is like is to think about your current organisation and something you have always said to yourself 'really needs to be changed'. Perhaps something that would help the organisation and its people work harder or smarter or both. It may be your current (external) clients consistently give you feedback about the organisation which you share, but the 'same old problems recur'. One reason the *status quo* remains may be that nobody but you knows of the problem; or the Board see it as of no importance; or the cost of change is seen as prohibitive. Whatever the cause the challenge for you is to present it as an opportunity and sell the benefits. You should do this in the form of a proposal in line with the framework explored in Chapter Three. You will need to include:

- factual information concerning the organisation that is needed to carry out the project;
- information concerning the resources you need;
- your understanding of what the project will mean to the client and impact upon the organisation as a whole.

Do this very much as a real exercise. Try and put yourself in the shoes of a consultant pitching to win business. Review your knowledge of your organisation and its people. The proposal needs to focus on:

the sponsor – who might align behind this proposal?

the client   – who is the buyer: the Board, MD, Purchasing Manager?

the issue   – although the 'problem' may show up as, say, poor cash flow management, is this really the issue?

the benefits – are they quantifiable or intangible? How will they be assessed? What will 'success' look like?

If this task excites and makes you eager for the challenge of consulting, all well and good. However, you will now need to explore whether there is a wider consultancy market than this one project.

Table 9.1   The market for consultancy – issues to consider

Issue	Considerations
• How much does your organisation spend each year on consultants?	• The amount may surprise you but read the points below with care.
• What is the range of work undertaken by external consultants?	• Is this vital 'expert' work or more routine 'turn-key' activity. How often are they used?
• What is the organisation's experience of consultants	• History can prove a valuable pointer to future experience; minimal use of consultants may indicate problems in identifying a legitimate role.
• What level of satisfaction is there with the services provided?	• This may be anecdotal. Would a survey help you capture ideas/concerns?
• What type of consultants are used?	• In other words is the focus on international strategy houses or a freelancer from the local college or what?
• What are the strengths and weaknesses of these consultants?	For example • calibre of staff • coverage of services by type or geography • service • fees
• What opportunities are there for internal consultancy?	• What changes are facing the organisation? • Where could an internal consultant 'make the difference' and add value? • How well has technology/learning from previous consultancy projects been absorbed by/transferred into your organisation?

Table 9.1 Continued

• Is there a sponsor?	• How dissatisfied are senior managers with current arrangements? • What benefits would appeal to them?
	• Who are the current 'buyers' of consultancy? Are there any others?
• What is the range of services you could offer now?	• How closely does this reflect the current use of consultants? • Are the areas in which you wish to operate in growth or decline?
• Fees	• What basis will you use? e.g. transfer pricing • How will you assess the competitiveness of your fee structure?

YOUR MARKET

Whatever your enthusiasm and skills is there a market for you? Or is your first challenge to use your skills to create an awareness of the need? In either event the framework in Table 9.1 is designed to get you thinking realistically about this.

TESTING THE INTERNAL MARKET

Having reviewed the questions above you may discover that you have only a partial view of the 'internal market' for your services; if so some market testing is called for. You should make contact with the major users of external consultants in your organisation. Ideally you should interview each one to explore the thinking behind their buying decisions, their satisfaction with the service provided, and their views on buying from an internal provider. The following questions will elicit the information required. If you cannot meet people face to face consider the use of a questionnaire based on Fig. 9.2.

CONSULTANT ASSESSMENT

BACKGROUND DETAILS

Consultancy
Nature of work
Duration of project
Fees
Expenses
Number of consultants used
Why were they chosen (e.g. expertise, reputation, price, quality of presentations etc.)?
How were they chosen (e.g. open competition, beauty parade etc.)?

OVERALL

- How well did they fulfil the terms of reference?
- Did results meet your expectations?
- Rate the benefits to the organisation as a whole.

PROGRESS

- How well did presentations meet your needs?
- Did they keep to their budget?
- Was the project completed on schedule?

QUALITY OF SERVICE

- How responsive were they to your needs?
- Give an assessment of your overall level of comfort with reports on progress, changes to schedule etc.
- Did they give you value for money?
- Would you use them again? Why?

INTERNAL CONSULTANCY

- In what areas would you consider using internal consultants?
- What benefits would using an internal consultant bring? What drawbacks?
- What would be the top three considerations in choosing to use an internal consultant?

The responses to these questions will help you determine how realistic your plans are. They should certainly provide pointers on areas in which there may be a latent but unrecognised need for your services.

Fig. 9.2 Sample consultant assessment questionnaire

Differentiating yourself

Your market survey will provide invaluable information on what potential buyers are looking for. This may not be consistent with what you see as your own strengths, so some choices will need to be made about the type of consultancy you can realistically offer. Table 9.2 shows the more common decisions that need to be taken.

Tailored versus packaged?

Here the choice is between providing bespoke solutions or packaged, off-the-shelf products. As with all these choices the approach adopted will reflect your own skills and the needs of your particular market.

Clients

Will you focus on specific clients, for example all your organisation's IT managers or market to all managers in the organisation? Or will you focus selectively on divisional managing directors?

Price

Pricing your services will require care. Large external practices need to be aware of the impact of differential pricing for different jobs within the same client and be prepared to defend it. There may be a wide variety of explanations: the seniority/experience of the staff, the complexity of the work, the 'market rate' in a particular specialism, or maybe colleagues forgot to liaise with each other.

Your research will tell you whether price sensitivity is a major issue. As an internal consultant you will certainly be expected to come in at very competitive rates.

How much innovation?

Are your skills in the strategic exploitation of IT? Or are you an experienced logistics manager who can harness IT to produce gains for your clients? There may be a perception from potential clients

Table 9.2 The market for consultancy – what should you offer?

Tailored	or	Packaged
Target clients	or	Wide-ranging client base
Fixed price	or	Price elasticity
Conventional	or	'Blue sky', hi-tech
Comprehensive	or	Selective
Expert or Specialist or Generalist		

that a major benefit of internal consultants would be 'a safe pair of hands that knows us', rather than a provider of leading edge thinking.

Coverage

The issue of comprehensive versus selective coverage is similar to that of tailored versus packaged solutions. Are you going to act as a focus for a complete range of consultancy services or work within selected markets – for example, human resources?

Expert, Specialist, or Generalist?

Having reviewed your own skills and planned for the acquisition of new ones you will need to think very carefully about this. One team of internal consultants was not seen as 'expert' until they competed for, and won, work in other organisations!

If you start off offering 'all things to all clients' you may get the reputation as a provider of low-level assistance on day-to-day issues rather than position yourself as a top-level adviser to senior management.

Making your case

Having made some decisions about the market and your role within it you should review the strength of your business case and put together a business plan. Fig. 9.3 is an example.

This will be a key document and will need to be persuasive and backed up by compelling benefits. You will need to identify a high-level sponsor within the organisation, someone who can see the benefits of an internal approach, and test out your proposition with them.

MAKING IT HAPPEN

To conclude, you have made your decision, your business plan has been supported, and you're in business! As in any new job there will be surprises and frustrations during the first few months. Here are a number of the most common:

Feast or famine?

'The first six months were fantastic' said the freelance consultant, 'however the next six were a near disaster'. The cause: paradoxically a loyal client! This consultant's first job had been a big one, so much so that the steps so vital to safeguarding your medium-term future, networking, marketing, and client contact, simply did not happen. This may be an extreme case but the cycle of an apparent excess of leads and 'almost more work than I can handle' is often followed by a period of famine. An effective marketing plan can help reduce the impact of this phenomenon. Indeed, you may wish to consider the times of year when things may be slack and build marketing activities into the 'window'. The Christmas and New Year period would be a case in point.

Independence versus client expectations

Working for yourself can be a very liberating experience. You have control over what you want to do and when you want to do it? Or do

Section	Purpose
• Situational Analysis	To present relevant *background* information and trends with their *implications and assumptions* for the future. Specifically in the internal market for consultancy.
• S.W.O.T. Analysis	To summarise the main issues: EXTERNAL: *Opportunities and Threats* – e.g. over-reliance on external expertise INTERNAL: *Strengths and Weaknesses* of providing internal consultancy services – e.g. development of in-house expertise; value for money.
• Objectives	To quantify the key measurable performance criteria – e.g. volume of business, value, profit and share of internal consultancy market.
• Strategies	To outline the ways which you intend to achieve your objectives; what services you will be offering, at what price.
• Action Plans (e.g. marketing)	To specify: – *What* will be done? – *Who* will do it and be responsible? – *When* will it be done? – *How much* will it cost?
• Profit & Loss Projections	To provide a cost and return summary over the next 3–5 years – i.e. the financial pay off from the plan.
• Controls	To ensure that the plan has a reviewable element and is therefore a *dynamic* document. To outline performance criteria and contingency measures.

Fig. 9.3 Factors to consider in business plan

you? You now have **clients** to serve and this means responsiveness to their needs and absolute responsibility for ensuring targets are met and quality maintained. And if you have moved from a line management role you may well be surprised by the seemingly trivial things that you now have to do. This may range from proof checking corrections to a proposal, to arranging the printing of covers for a report, or setting up a training room for a workshop.

Preparing your marketing literature

The lesson here seems to be to have something of the **right quality** available very quickly. A major task in the short term will be to engage the interest of potential clients. Your survey of your operation's use of consultants may well give some valuable pointers as to the benefits that are being looked for. But without a 'brochure' your audience may not take your claims seriously. Moreover, a brochure gives your colleagues something tangible to discuss with their peers: comments such as 'seen this, it's impressive, I really would like to use our own people' are an invaluable marketing ally. Get some professional help with the design of your material – a document that looks 'old fashioned' or produced 'on the cheap' will convey just that impression of your consulting services.

Standing alone

Integrity and independence are virtues we all value. In your first few months you may feel pangs of regret that you have given up membership of a team for a professional role where you must at once be an impartial provider of a service yet still a member of the organisation in the widest sense. This can impose a loneliness in the short term with no colleagues with whom to brainstorm ideas or test out your thinking. The need here is to network with fellow consultants outside the organisation. They will all have been through the same ups and downs and can provide a powerful sense of balance. You will also have to get used to explaining to former colleagues what your role now is.

Follow up your leads!

We explored the opportunities for selling on in Chapter Four. Remember that if you excite a potential client's interest they will expect a follow-up. A delay of weeks may well cost you the opportunity. Surprisingly perhaps, these delays do occur usually because of poor time management by the consultant. Another cause is that some consultants are very action-focused and derive most satisfaction from pitching for business and actually conducting their project rather than writing proposals. However, without proposals you will not get the opportunity to practise your consulting skills, so keep writing.

Information is power!

As an internal consultant you need to know what is going on in your organisation, and what is likely to occur in the future. Remember therefore to keep yourself on distribution lists to ensure you receive business circulars. Don't ignore the internal network, formal and informal.

Knowledge is power!

Just as focusing on your internal market is important, so is keeping abreast of trends in your sector or industry. Many of your clients will particularly value a perspective that goes wider than their own experience. Indeed this may be the prime reason for using consultants. So think about subscriptions to professional bodies and journals.

Value your services appropriately

There is a risk that in your eagerness to establish your reputation, you will seriously underestimate the benefits your assistance can produce. Thus a 'free' investigatory survey may send a message to your client that such things are relatively easy to conduct. In reality they may make heavy demands on your professional skills.

Client reaction to a free lunchtime seminar offered by a large consultancy was to the effect that 'if it's free it must just be a marketing stunt; I'm more than happy to pay £250 for an event that helps my thinking but I doubt if this event will do that'. The consultancy in question misread the perception the event would create in their clients' eyes. Future events were beefed up with a case study and marketed at £350! You will not be surprised to learn that they were a success Should this appear to be exploitation of the client, the research which went into the event and the advice which was offered was of considerable value.

Don't ignore the paperwork

In the excitement of 'doing the business' – i.e. working with and for your clients, some consultants ignore the basics of good house-keeping. The result: incorrect fee notes, missed meetings, cash flow problems . . .

Invest time in yourself

Consulting is a process of continuous learning. You will have considerable opportunities to learn from your experience. However, you must also acknowledge that some learning can best be accomplished by other means. For professionals committed to helping others learn, consultants can be surprisingly lax about expanding their own knowledge. So build training and development events into your plans. Commit to attend appropriate conferences, training programmes etc. and do you best to attend.

On a personal basis you must also ask yourself about the impact of work on your life outside work. If you are working upwards of 60 hours a week, ask yourself why?

- is it absolutely necessary to accomplish vital goals?
- do long hours really help you do this, or does your productivity go down over an extended time?
- do you take pride in working long hours?
- are long hours a source of stress to you?
- are your long hours a source of stress to other people – your family, or your subordinates?

You should consider the maxims of 'working smarter not harder' and 'assessment by results, not effort'. Following these can help to avoid the activity trap which some consultants fall into, when simply 'being there' is equated with being effective.

Learn from your successes

At some point in your consulting career things may go wrong. Try and start out with a belief that there is no such word as 'failure', rather, opportunities to continuously do better. And when things go well, as they surely will, practise positive debriefing. Review what worked and why. This is a particularly important aspect for the preservation of personal self-esteem, since every time you propose, intervene, and recommend as a consultant you are giving of yourself.

INDEX